"Theology, that deep und ~~...~~ ...us ways, has fallen on hard times in the Church today. One reason is that Christians are lazy and satisfied with a shallow understanding of God built on clichés and misconceptions so popular today. Stephen exposes many of those common clichés and challenges us to look to the Scriptures and dig deeply for a proper understanding of biblical truth. Let this book move you to look to the Scriptures for answers rather than repeating the meaningless mantras we have accepted for too long."

TIMOTHY A. PASMA, SENIOR PASTOR
LA RUE BAPTIST CHURCH, LA RUE, OHIO

"How surprising and refreshing this book is! In a culture where critical thinking is not the norm in many of our pulpits and pews, Stephen has provided us with a good reason to put down the remote and pick up our responsibility to interact with a sovereign Creator who wants us to know Him and His blessed Word. I highly recommend this thought-provoking little book."

DAVID CARLYLE, SENIOR PASTOR
FITE MEMORIAL BAPTIST CHURCH, MARION, OHIO

"*Defying Ignorance* is a call for the Church to abandon its man-centered approach and to return to a God-centered, scriptural approach to life and truth. This book is written to ordinary Christians who are open to re-examining the biblical basis for some of their long held beliefs."

JIM NEWHEISER, SENIOR PASTOR
GRACE BIBLE CHURCH, ESCONDIDO, CALIFORNIA

"*Defying Ignorance* is a refreshing representation about many of the slogans that litter biblical Christianity. Conversations among Christians and non-Christians alike are inundated with rhetoric that has little to no scriptural background. Such phraseology is frequently ascribed as "Thus saith the Lord." Stephen Hill exposes the scriptural accuracy of several contemporary clichés that characterize our age. *Defying Ignorance* will bring edification to any Christian and will be a helpful resource in dialoguing with those who have shaped their understanding around church folklore."

DR. BRENT BREWER, PASTOR
TRINITY REFORMED BAPTIST CHURCH,
JOPPA, MARYLAND

"Years ago, I watched in awe as Buster Douglas pounded away at the popular world heavy weight champion, Mike Tyson, and removed him from his throne of domination. Now, years later, I'm privileged to witness the same pummeling as Stephen Hill takes on the false ideologies that have found their way into Christendom and influenced so many Christians. *Defying Ignorance* is a real knock out blow to the satanic dominion that reigns in many circles today. There is no doubt that this book will shock the world of saints as it reveals how many half-truths have entered into our ranks."

DR. KEITH A. SHERLIN
PROFESSOR, TYNDALE THEOLOGICAL SEMINARY
PASTOR, NEW BEGINNINGS BIBLE CHURCH
FOUNDER, ESSENTIAL CHRISTIANITY MINISTRIES

"Many years ago a well-known theologian reminded me that to be biblical we must hold to a theology of the second-glance (a deeper and more reflective biblical assessment of commonly accepted evangelical sayings or interpretations). He was referring, of course, to those many popular evangelical vignettes floating around today that are biblically deficient examples of a theology of the first-glance (scripturally unchecked and emotionally accepted sayings or interpretations). Stephen's book moves us toward cultivating a theology of the second-glance by scripturally dismantling those dangerous vignettes and paving a clear way toward maturity."

JERRY MARCELLINO
PASTOR, AUDUBON DRIVE BIBLE CHURCH
DIRECTOR, AUDUBON PRESS &
CHRISTIAN BOOK SERVICE
MODERATOR, FELLOWSHIP OF INDEPENDENT
REFORMED EVANGELICALS

DEFYING IGNORANCE

*Exposing Christianity's
Most Popular Myths*

STEPHEN HILL

PublishAmerica
Baltimore

ISBN: 1-60441-554-1
PUBLISHED BY PUBLISHAMERICA, LLLP
www.publishamerica.com
Baltimore

Printed in the United States of America

"For the time will come when men will not put up with sound doctrine. Instead, to suit their own desires, they will gather around them a great number of teachers to say what their itching ears want to hear. They will turn their ears away from the truth and turn aside to myths."

—2 Timothy 4:3-4

Contents

Introduction

My revelation was a mild one. God's methods of conversion or enlightenment have been so powerful and intense for some prophets, apostles, and reformers that they've gone down in history, resonating in our hearts and permeating the very fabric of our souls.

But God's methods were different with me. Different, but just as powerful. Not like Paul's conversion on the road to Damascus, or Luther's battle amidst a fierce lightning storm, or even R. C. Sproul's humbling encounter with his Creator that forced him out of bed and to his knees in a chapel in the middle of the night. No, my revelation was not something you would find in a movie, a novel, or a fairy tale. It was not an event that left me paralyzed or breathless, nor was it an occurrence that kept me from sleeping at night. Mine came about over a cup of coffee and a hot Bob Evans breakfast in the little town of Marion, Ohio.

The morning of my awakening was no different from any other morning. My wife and I met our friend Tom for an early breakfast, which we enjoyed because the conversation was always great, and the strawberry pancakes weren't half bad either. Tom and I were two peas in a pod, lovers of debate and always yearning for a deeper understanding of God's nature. This often meant profound theological discussions over topics or terms that most Christians aren't even aware of, much less talk about. Dispensationalism, theonomy, cessationism and continuationism, pedobaptism and credobaptism, vincible and invincible ignorance are just a few examples of the topics that frequented our discussions and kept the thick-treaded wheels of our minds turning.

I got a kick out of watching our friends react to our talks. Their facial expressions spoke a thousand words, as they conjured up images of us sitting in high backed, wooden chairs, adorned in robes and smoking bent pipes. Most of them grew so bored with how scholarly our conversations sounded that they couldn't stomach even being in the same room. I don't blame them. I get tired of hearing myself at times. I can only imagine what it must be like for someone else to sit through my tiring lectures. Nonetheless, Tom and I enjoyed nothing more than a fiery debate over the most complex issues we could muster up, and this morning was no different.

Up till this morning our discussions had always been intriguing, but this day was about to bring a whirlwind of change that I was completely unprepared for and that hit me with a Hiroshima-sized spiritual blast.

I had been a professing Christian for years. I grew up in the church, was baptized when I was only twelve, and from that point forward never doubted my salvation or spiritual maturity.

Tom was the complete opposite. He was a recent convert and had come to know the Lord as a college student at Ohio University.

Before he accepted Christ, Tom was the textbook example

of a hoodlum. He partied, drank, did drugs, had sex, and led a life of total disregard for everything holy. Had he lived in Christ's time, he would have undoubtedly been a tax collector, only with more friends than the average tax collector.

Needless to say, his conversion was remarkable, and a living testament to God's mercy, power, and grace in transforming even the most wretched sinner into a faithful servant to His will.

Tom steadily grew in his faith through the encouragement of Christian friends at the university and at home. While at home, he attended a Pentecostal church pastored by one of our close, albeit older, brothers in Christ. At school, he attended a different church with his good friend Mark, who later became a missionary to China. This church was very different from the Pentecostal one he attended at home. It was a Baptist church with a Reformed pastor and was much more conservative than the charismatic style he was used to from home.

As he was at school more often than home, the Baptist church became his home church and the place he really grew in. But approaching graduation and a move back home, the Baptist church would no longer be an option because it was simply too far away. So, he talked with the pastor of the church, who happened to be from our home town of Marion himself, and asked if there were any particular churches he would recommend. Without hesitation, he recommended La Rue Baptist, where he grew up.

Tom heeded his pastor's advice and tested the waters at La Rue. A few weeks later, over a tasty breakfast at Bob Evans, he shared with me what he was learning.

As we sat down in our booth, I could tell Tom was eager to share something with me. He had a glimmer in his eye, much like a five-year-old who just got a new toy that will occupy hours of his time for the next few weeks and drive his parents crazy. He was fidgety, as though he would soon burst if he didn't say what it was he wanted to say. No sooner did the words "I'll put that order right in for you" utter from our waitress's lips, than did Tom say, "Steve, I'm learning so much at La Rue, and I've *got* to share it with you!"

Confident that Tom couldn't possibly share anything with me that I didn't already know from my years of experience as a believer, I half-heartedly replied, "Sure, go ahead," and quietly muttered to my wife under my breath, "This should be interesting."

He began by explaining that La Rue Baptist's pastor, a man named Timothy Pasma, preached in an expositional style, meaning he taught verse by verse, dissecting each bit of Scripture and explaining its meaning. This method was also exegetical; that is, it critically analyzed the text, often from the original Greek and Hebrew, to ensure accurate interpretation and ultimately the most correct understanding of God's Word.

With that disclaimer, Tom lit the spark that would ignite the most fiery debate we would ever have. He proceeded to systematically disarm my entire understanding of God, turning nearly everything I'd always been taught in the church right on its head. Calvinism was the dominant topic of conversation and a foe I was not prepared to battle.

What Tom shared with me was an understanding of God that was radically different from anything I'd ever known, and quite frankly, far from what I ever wanted to believe. I was confident that I could pull verse after verse out of my biblical arsenal to defend my views and shoot down Tom's absurd new notions of the Lord, but much to my dismay, I found my arsenal empty.

Tom's on the other hand, was quite full. In fact, his was shock-in-awe caliber, and he proved his points scripturally, verse after verse after verse.

I frantically searched my Bible, hoping to find at least a shred of evidence to prove my case, but all I found was the opposite. Nearly everything I read screamed Calvinism, but I wasn't ready to give in quite yet.

While I sat flipping through the thin pages of my thick, tattered Bible, Tom sat snickering, twiddling his thumbs in childlike satisfaction.

"I'll give you as much time as you need," Tom kindly offered. "A day, a month, a year, a decade... Just tell me how long you need, and I'll wait. If you come back to me with solid scriptural proof, I'll take back everything I've said today."

Sensing his blatant sarcasm, I quickly realized that Tom's overblown confidence stemmed from the fact that no matter how much time I spent searching for verses to support my argument, I would never find any because *they aren't there*. Oh, I certainly thought they were because I'd been made to believe they were for years. Surely my pastor would never lie to me about what is and isn't in God's Word. My own parents wouldn't steer me down a path of deceit and lead me to believe something that was completely untrue. My Christian friends wouldn't persuade me to think the Bible says something it doesn't.

But it happened nonetheless.

How did it happen, though? How could such educated, knowledgeable, mature Christians make such a grievous mistake?

I'll tell you how: they heard it their whole lives and took for granted it was all true just like I did.

Still, that didn't make me feel any better. After my embarrassment from being defeated so shamefully by Tom subsided, a more crippling feeling set in. I could swallow my pride for losing an argument, but I could not accept that I had believed lies about my faith for so many years. I felt jipped, like I was a toy that had been maliciously manipulated by an evil puppet master.

But now the strings were broken. I was set free and suddenly saw everything in a new and blinding light. For me, the truths of Calvinism are what broke my chains, but for some the mere recognition of even the smallest biblical truth can evoke a powerful, life-changing experience.

The intent of this book is not to make an argument for Calvinism, although I recommend many authors and books if you wish to experience the same revelation I did that morning. R. C. Sproul's *Chosen by God, The Holiness of God,* and *What is Reformed Theology?* are all incredible books on Reformed Theology. John Piper's works are also excellent, along with Kris Lundgaard's *The Enemy Within,* which is a modern recreation of John Owen's work *The Mortification of Sin.* Classic Reformation authors and works include Martin Luther's *The Bondage of the Will,* Jonathon Edwards' *Freedom of the Will,* and John Bunyan's *Pilgrim's Progress,* to name a few. A great website for Reformed Theology is monergism.com, and all these books and many more can be read on the site or purchased from its online bookstore.

But back to the purpose of this book...

After conceding to Tom, I resorted to the oldest trick I knew—my last resort, the one card always left tucked in my sleeve in case I needed it for the most desperate of emergencies. This one had to work.

"Well, you may be right," I humbly admitted to Tom, "but all that really matters is that we both know the Lord."

Did you see it coming? How many times have you heard that one? Or have you even used it yourself a time or two?

Tom's response to my common copout was gentle, but not quite what I was hoping for.

"Yes and no," he replied. "What we discussed today isn't salvific; that is, it doesn't determine our salvation, but it most certainly changes the way we know and understand God, and *that* is what helps us to grow spiritually."

In that moment, I realized that Tom was one hundred percent right. The theological debates we often had never dealt with anything directly related to our salvation, but they drastically affected our understanding of God, which ultimately determined how well we *knew* God. In other words, the more we understand our Father, the better we know Him, and the better our relationship with Him ultimately is.

So many Christians today seem content with saying "I am saved and that's all that matters." They have no desire to learn more about the one who saved them. They view the moment of their salvation as an ending point rather than a starting point.

We are commanded in Philippians 2:12 to work out our salvation with fear and trembling. Our spiritual journey is one riddled with trials, according to James 1, that ultimately produce endurance and maturity. It is a process of sanctification, whereby God continually molds us into the vessels He wants us to be, not mere puppets dangling by the threads of ignorance. By faith, those threads will be broken, and God will grant us wisdom we never thought possible.

That is the purpose of this book. By taking a closer look at the most common biblical misconceptions of modern Christianity and discovering the truth behind them, we will no longer be fooled as I was into believing something that isn't true; but more importantly, we will grow in our understanding of our wonderful Savior and hopefully grow abundantly in Him.

As you read through each chapter, think carefully about how many times these common fallacies have fooled you. Don't be content with simply taking my word for it. That's exactly how we are fooled into believing deceptions in the first place. Take time to thoroughly study each chapter's topic and take notes on what you read. My challenge will be what Tom's was to me. Take as much time as you need to prove the validity of each chapter's statement, but when you discover that the statements are misleading, I pray that your realization will be as life-altering as mine was that blessed Bob Evans morning.

1 | *"All Sins Are Equal in the Eyes of God"*

If you've been a church-going Christian for more than a year, chances are you've heard the phrase "all sins are equal in the eyes of God" spoken by more people, more times than you can count. Indeed, this phrase has been so loosely thrown around that most Christians take for granted that it's not only true, but that it is an actual verse, taken straight from the Bible, verbatim, with such poignancy that no person could ever deny its truth or existence.

But have you ever taken the time to look it up yourself? If so, you've discovered that the phrase "all sins are equal in the eyes of God" cannot be found anywhere in the Bible and is, according to Scripture, only partially true.

All sins *are* equal in one sense: they are all equal in their ability to condemn and to separate us from God:

> But your iniquities have separated you from your God; your sins have hidden His face from you, so that He will not hear. (Isaiah. 59:2)

> They are darkened in their understanding and
> separated from the life of God because of the
> ignorance that is in them due to the hardening of
> their hearts. (Ephesians 4:18)

As a perfect God, holy and righteous in every way, no sin, no matter how small, is acceptable in His eyes. God is so pure that every iniquity is detestable to Him. In the absence of Christ's redemptive work on the cross, which paid the penalty for all sins, big and small, stealing a piece of gum would damn a soul to Hell for all eternity the same way rape or murder would. And as fallen human beings, born into sin, we can't help but commit all kinds of trespasses against God, no matter how hard we may try not to. Romans 3: 10-18 is a foundational passage for the doctrine of depravity and paints a clear picture of the innate wickedness of mankind:

> As it is written: "There is no one righteous, not
> even one; there is no one who understands, no one
> who seeks God. All have turned away, they have
> together become worthless; there is no one who
> does good, not even one. Their throats are open
> graves; their tongues practice deceit. The poison
> of vipers is on their lips. Their mouths are full of
> cursing and bitterness. Their feet are swift to shed
> blood; ruin and misery mark their ways, and the
> way of peace they do not know. There is no fear of
> God before their eyes." (Romans 3:10-18)

Not even one, we read, is righteous. We then read later in verse 23 of the same chapter "for all have sinned and fall short of the glory of God."

If not even one person does good, then all sin. And if all sin, then we know by default that all sin is equally deserving of the same fate in light of the glory and majesty of the Most High God. If one thing is scripturally clear, it is that all people are in need of Christ's atonement for their sins to gain entrance into God's kingdom. All sin, no matter how small or insignificant, requires atonement through Christ.

But what about the severity of different sins? Most Christians who throw the "all sins are equal" phrase around use it as fuel for an argument that no sin is worse than any other. They argue that since God hates all sin equally, no one sin is any more grievous than another.

I remember a conversation I had with a friend from church years ago. I was in college at the time, and this friend who had heard the same fundamental teachings I had growing up, admitted to having pre-marital sex and feeling as though he did nothing wrong.

Appalled by his lack of penitence, I rebuked him and urged him to repent and to turn from a sin that he saw as no big deal. His justification for not feeling guilty was that "all sins are equal in the eyes of God, so who cares if I have pre-marital sex or step on an ant?"

Are you beginning to see the problem with this warped way of thinking? My friend saw nothing wrong with committing even the worst of sins because his understanding of Scripture afforded him the belief that no sin is any worse than any other. To him, murder wouldn't have been any worse than swearing or forgetting to say "excuse me" after a loud belch at the dinner table.

This interpretation of the equality of sins cheapens God's holy mandates, and such an act is so dangerous that no person in his right mind would ever dare commit it. But let's look at what Scripture says about the severity of different sins.

The Law, given by God to Moses for His people, set forth the Lord's parameters for Godly living and the punishments for breaching those parameters. God warns His people countless times in books of the Old Testament to obey His laws— especially Exodus, Leviticus, Numbers, and Deuteronomy. He also brings about swift punishment to those who do not obey His commands:

> They will pay for their sins because they rejected my laws and abhorred my decrees. (Leviticus 26:43)

Do the Great Flood or Sodom and Gomorrah ring a bell?

The Law, decreed by God Himself, assigned different punishments to different sins, according to the degree of each sin. The punishment for murder was death, while the punishment for stealing and false swearing was banishment (Zechariah 5:3). No one would deny that a murderer's punishment was much harsher than the punishment for a common thief. And let's not forget that it is God who imposed these varying levels of punishment.

Still, the New Covenant fulfilled the Law in Christ's redemptive work on the cross. God promised, "I will put my laws in their hearts, and I will write them on their minds" (Hebrews 10:16). Because of grace, we are no longer slaves to sin or the Law, but does that change the fact that certain sins are more severe and detrimental than others?

Perhaps the best evidence that not all sins are equal in magnitude comes from Jesus himself. In John 19:11, Jesus responds to a plea from Pilate to speak. When Pilate reminds Jesus that he has the power to release Him or to have Him crucified, Jesus boldly informs Pilate, "You would have no power over me if it were not given to you from above. Therefore the one who handed me over to you is guilty of a *greater* sin."

The first time I read this passage with full alertness was during a Bible study. The topic at hand had nothing to do with varying levels of sin, but upon reading the passage I asked the study leader to pause momentarily so we could discuss the verse. Every single member of the Bible study—many very wise, spiritually mature men—were dumbfounded by Jesus' statement of a sin being "greater" because that notion seemed to completely contradict everything we had all learned about sin. Needless to say, we all left that week's study perplexed but determined to discover the truth and share it the following week.

As I researched the issue further on my own, God graciously revealed to me that sins are equal in their damning quality, but not in their severity. All sins are unworthy of our pure, holy, perfect Father and are equally deserving of a damnable fate. Sins are not all equal in their severity, however, which Jesus Himself made clear to Pilate, and which we see in God's original Law to the Jews.

Furthermore, the earthly repercussions for some sins are far worse than others. Someone who receives a speeding ticket is required by the law to pay a simple fine and often doesn't even see the inside of a court room, whereas a serial killer may be sentenced to the death penalty and killed for his crimes. In the same way, a follower of Christ will most assuredly suffer more from committing a worse sin, as his convictions will be much greater than if he had committed a smaller, less significant offense.

The most egregious sin, the unpardonable sin, is itself yet another example of the varying degrees of iniquity. Jesus

remarks in Matthew 12:31 that "every sin and blasphemy will
be forgiven men, but the blasphemy against the Spirit will not
be forgiven." Jesus singles out one sin that is so severe that it
may never be forgiven, in this life or the next. Such a sin is
clearly worse than any other in its severity. If other sins were of
the same caliber, Jesus would have deemed them unforgivable
as well.

Thank God that as Christians the Law is written on our
hearts and minds. God has made the wages of sin and the
differences between good and evil abundantly clear to us
through His Word and the Holy Spirit. To conveniently
interpret the equality of sin to mean that no sins are worse than
others is a gross negligence of what God has made known to us.

Through our convictions we know that while all sin is evil,
some sins are worse than others, simply by their effect on our
conscience if nothing else. To feel no remorse for committing
greater sin, as my friend did, is a copout and an excuse to
continue living a life of rebellion against God. On the other
hand, realizing that evil comes in many shapes and sizes
heightens our convictions, brings us to penitence, and
ultimately leads to healing.

While the statement this chapter deals with is partially true,
it is not entirely true from a biblical perspective. God's Word
provides inarguable proof that while all sins are equal in one
sense, they are not equal in the other. The Law clearly
distinguished different sins by providing harsher punishments
for worse sins. Jesus cited the Pharisees' sin as a "greater" sin
compared to Pilate's and deemed one sin the worst of all by
labeling it the only unforgivable sin. Every sin is just as
deserving of an eternity in Hell as the unpardonable sin when
weighed against God's infinite holiness, but the magnitude of
every other iniquity pales in comparison to that one sin.

When Christians quote the popular phrase "all sins are equal in the eyes of God," they should be careful to state exactly what they mean. Do they mean to point out that no sin is any more pleasing to God than any other or that no sin is any more egregious than another? There is a world of difference between those philosophies, and the former is accurate while the latter is dangerously misleading. The most accurate pronouncement of the popular phrase would be, "All sins are and aren't equal in the eyes of God," but seeing as that change won't likely come about any time in the near future, we're left with our own understanding of the equality of sin.

The next time you hear someone say "all sins are equal in the eyes of God" as if it were quoted straight from the Bible, make it a point to ask them what they mean. And if you find your friend in confusion, gently set the record straight.

Questions for Reflection

1. Before reading this chapter, did you believe that the phrase "all sins are equal in the eyes of God" was a Bible verse? If so, how do you feel now that you know it's not?

2. When you've thought about the equality of sin or heard it mentioned, was it in relation to the nature of sin or its level of severity?

3. How does the reality that some sins are worse than others in God's eyes shape your understanding of sin and your relationship with God?

4. Have you ever used the equality of sin as justification for committing a worse sin? If so, will you do it again?

2 | *"We Are All the Children of God"*

How many times have you heard the coined slogan "we are all the children of God?" Probably even more times than the popular phrase of the previous chapter. Why? Because the equality of sin is a topic that Christians will breach but that unbelievers typically don't care to deal with.

God's love and acceptance, and His role as Father to the whole world, however, are something entirely different. Christians and non-Christians alike have no problem addressing the topic of God's love or His divine role as Creator because these notions are so universally accepted that discussing them is commonplace. Compared to other theological conundrums, these fields of study are much less controversial and much more comfortable to tackle.

There are inarguably different kinds of professing Christians in the world. There are those who love the Gospel of Jesus Christ and devote their lives to Godly living, servitude, humility, and the eagerness to learn more about their Maker in an effort to become increasingly holy. There are those who attend church on a near-weekly basis because they think it is the right thing to do or the most appropriate place to raise their children with values. There are others who are comically referred to as "Chreaster Christians" who attend church only on major holidays, like Christmas and Easter as their alias suggests, because they claim to recognize the importance of paying dues to God from time to time. And finally, there are those "Christians" who simply profess to believe in God, but that's about the extent of their dedication to Christ. This latter group often call themselves "spiritual," as opposed to "religious" as if to protest their dissatisfaction with doctrine or other religious impositions that they feel hinder a pleasant, less threatening view of God.

You will be hard pressed to find a Christian from the first group who makes the claim "we are all the children of God." Some from the second group will, and more from the "Chreaster" group, and still more from the "spiritual" group, and often times even unbelievers will make the claim; but not one from the first group would make that claim. Why? Because the total opposite is explicit in the Bible.

Let's take a close look at three verses to get a better grasp on what renders us "children of God:"

> In other words, it is not the natural children who are God's children, but it is the children of the promise who are regarded as Abraham's offspring. (Romans 9:8)

> This is how we know who the children of God are and who the children of the devil are: Anyone who does not do what is right is not a child of God; nor is anyone who does not love his brother. (1 John 3:10)

We know that we are children of God, and that the whole world is under the control of the evil one. (1 John 5:19)

According to Romans 9:8, one criteria for being a child of God is to be a child of the promise. What in the world does that mean? you might ask. What does God mean by "natural" children versus children of the "promise?"

Predicting the same response from the Romans, Paul rhetorically asks and then answers the same question. The promise, he points out in verse nine, refers to God's promise that Sarah would have a son. Isaac, then, is a clear child of the promise. In verses 10-13, Paul cites Jacob as another child of the promise, in sharp contrast to his brother, Esau:

> Yet before the twins were born or had done anything good or bad," God declared, "Jacob I loved, but Esau I hated." (Romans 9:11-13)

In both cases, Isaac and Jacob are children of God's promise—first to Sarah, then to Rebekah. But these cases apply to individuals. What about Christians today? God didn't promise my mother a son, so how do I know I am a child of the promise?

1 John 3:10 provides an explanation that applies to us all. John shoots us as straight as possible. "This is how you distinguish God's children from the children of the devil," he says: "the child of God does what is right and loves his brother, and the child of the devil does neither."

A couple chapters later, John reminds us that those who are part of the world, those who are natural born, or born of the flesh as Romans 9:8 describes them, are under the control of the evil one.

A clear distinction is made between God's children and the devil's. Paul and John provide specific qualifications for both groups and clearly distinguish between the two. The right to be called a child of God is reserved for a certain class of people. God grants this right to His chosen people, those who accept His free gift of salvation through His son. The rest of the world falls under a different, completely opposite category. Though they are created by God, they are not the *children* of God as God defines His children. They are the children of the evil one because they reject their Heavenly Father.

So often Christians confuse their nature as image bearers of God with their status as children of God. Indeed, God does create every life, and in His own image according to Genesis chapters 1 and 5. But He does not call all His creations His children.

This is a very confusing concept, to say the least, because as humans we reproduce and our children are inevitably ours. My two children are undeniably mine. Even if I didn't want to be their father, I would still be their father. That reality is inescapable for every human parent. Even a man who abandons his family and denies his children cannot escape the fact that he is their biological parent. (Just watch an episode of Maury Povich.) Likewise, children who abandon their parents cannot escape the reality that their parents are responsible for their existence. If my son or daughter ran away and avoided me like the plague, I would still be their father just as much as the day they were conceived or born.

But that is not so with God. Our parents give us life in a scientific sense, but it is God who forms us and truly gives us life. The Psalmist writes in chapter 139, verse 13, "For you created my inmost being; you knit me together in my mother's womb."

As our creator, God knows every minute detail about us. Indeed, He knows us better than we know ourselves. Jesus reminds us in Matthew 10:30 that "even the very hairs of [our heads] are all numbered."

The notion that people created by God are not all the children of God is a very confusing biblical truth, especially in light of God's intimate knowledge of everyone He creates. To make things simpler, let's compare our relationship with God to our relationships at work.

Just as God created us in His image, our employers train and lead us in our jobs. They mold us, in a sense, into the employees they want us to be. After receiving the training, many employees stay with their employers, but many others leave in pursuit of another career or just a life free from work.

Once an employee leaves, does she retain her title as an employee? Of course not, because she isn't working for her employer any longer. She may become the employee of someone else, but in the eyes of her original employer, her status as an employee no longer exists. She has been erased from the payroll, her desk has been cleared, and her flashy framed portrait has been taken off the wall.

Like the employer, God forms us and molds us into the people we are. Just as the employer hires his employees, God "hires" us in a sense when He draws us to redemption in Christ and commissions us to spread the Gospel throughout the world. In the same way the employer refers to his new hires as employees, God refers to those whom He calls as His children. But what about those who are created by God but not chosen by Him?

The employee who leaves may still retain her title as an employee, but not as an employee of her original employer. In the same sense, those who reject Christ are still children, but not *His* children. They are children of another father, employees of another boss, slaves to another master. They have relinquished the right to be called children of the living God in exchange for the right to be called children of the devil. They remain slaves to sin instead of servants to righteousness.

God creates all people, but only the righteous obtain the right to be called the children of God. Galations 3:18, Ephesians 1:14 and 18, Colossians 1:12 and 3:24, Hebrews 9:15, and 1 Peter 1:4 all refer to the "inheritance" awarded to all believers—an inheritance promised to all of God's children as they are adopted through Christ (Ephesians 1:5).

Because of Adam and Eve's original sin, we are all initially born into a life of sin and are naturally separated from God. We are totally depraved and in need of redemption to obtain an inheritance in the Kingdom of Heaven. Upon accepting Christ, God adopts us as His sons and daughters, grants us an eternal inheritance in His kingdom, and gives us the right to be called His children. This is a title to be proud of and one that God's true children should not be willing to share. "We are all God's creations" may be declared by every living creature on earth, but the phrase "we are all the children of God" should only be spoken amidst a body of believers.

Questions for Reflection

1. Who have you heard make the claim that "we are all the children of God?" You've likely heard many people say it, but would you describe most of them as spiritually mature or immature?

2. If everyone were a child of God, what special qualities would be afforded to Christians?

3. As a believer, God has granted you the special right to be called one of His children. How does that privilege make you feel? Do you feel better or worse knowing that your special title is not available to everyone?

3 | *"Hate the Sin, Love the Sinner"*

Before we delve into this one, let's take a look at what really constitutes God's love and hatred by defining both terms in a biblical context as they relate to God.

If I asked you what your favorite food is and you said "spaghetti," what would your response be if I asked you if you love spaghetti? If I asked you to name your favorite sports team and you said the Cleveland Indians, how would you reply if I asked if you loved the Indians? What about your parents? Your children? Would you say you love them?

What about God?

My guess is that your answer to all of these questions would be that yes, you do love all of these things, but as I'm sure you noticed in doing this short exercise, you would probably define "love" very differently in each of these contexts. This is precisely why it is so imperative to properly and narrowly define terms as you study theology.

When I discuss the "love" of God in this chapter, I am referring to God's benevolent love, which is characterized and defined by God's intent to use all of His power and good will to

34

make the objects of His love and grace happy for eternity. When I discuss the "hatred" of God, I am referring to God's fixed determination to punish the impenitent wicked in light of His righteous, perfect judgment. God's hatred, then, is the opposite of His love as I define both terms. It is not an evil, sinful passion, but is rather the absence of any benevolence, or kind will, directed at the sinner by God.

Both the love of God and the hatred of God are different in nature than the same attributes of man. As a human being, my loving God means that I act upon my need for Him. As a regenerated sinner, I need God the same way I need water or air to survive. I embrace all that God provides me as I humbly come before His throne of grace. My love for Him is rooted in my fundamental *need* for Him.

God, however, does not need me at all. The love that God bestows on me is an overflow of His incredible grace. He demonstrates His love for me by saving me when I don't deserve it and by using all of His power to graciously bring me into His presence and allow me to experience pure joy forever.

In contrast to love, my hatred as a human being is sinful. It is malicious, spiteful, and free of any compassion for the one it is directed towards. God's hatred, on the other hand, is not sinful or passionate, but is rather an exercise of His divine judgment. That is not to say that God's hatred doesn't involve emotion—it does. God possesses anger for those He justly hates and executes that anger through His wrath, but His motives are always just, never evil.

With these definitions of love and hatred in their appropriate contexts, I will begin analyzing the topic of this chapter. We just learned that as God's children we hold special favor, but does that special favor extend to a deeper love? Does God *love* all people or just His children?

Now before I continue, I need to make something very clear. Of all the myths I will discuss in this book, this is by far the one I wrestle with most. The early Reformers like Martin Luther, John Calvin, Jonathan Edwards, John Owen, and John Knox, to name a few, all asserted that God hates sinners and that divine hatred is an attribute of God. See http://www.cprf.co.uk/quotes/hatredreprobate.htm for a plethora of quotations from them and many more. Like most modern day Reformers, I tend to look to the teachings of our Reformation fathers to gain insight into theological truths, and in this particular case I have no choice but to agree with their philosophies. Still, I pondered over this one issue for hours trying to decide whether or not to even include it as part of this book, and after searching God's will in light of the aim of this book, I finally decided to include it.

That said, I will state for the record that while I have struggled with the notion that God does not love everyone, I am positive that the coined slogan that God "hates the sin and loves the sinner" is not a part of the Holy Bible.

Theologians have fought over this issue for centuries. Even Reformed theologians, who wholly accept the doctrines of depravity, grace, predestination, and eternal security, cannot agree on whether God's love extends to all creatures or just His elect.

The argument is, in fact, so controversial that there are two groups within Reformed Theology: five-point Calvinists and four-point Calvinists. The "points" refer to five pillars of Reformed doctrine, and as their group names suggest, five-point Calvinists adhere to all five, while four-point Calvinists adhere to only four.

The five points conveniently spell out the acronym TULIP, so they are easier to remember. Each letter is the first letter of a term that begins with an adjective.

The "T" stands for Total Depravity, which is the fundamental truth that according to Scripture all men are innately wicked and separate from God. The word *depraved* should not be confused with the word *deprived*. To be *deprived* is to be lacking of something. To be *depraved* is to be morally corrupt and perverted.

Depravity goes beyond our lack of righteousness and our need for Christ. It embodies our complete unworthiness—our evil, selfish nature that necessitates repentance and forgiveness of our sins. In light of the fall, total depravity means that even the best works of men are displeasing to God when weighed against His purity and standards for perfection. To understand the remaining points, we must first understand depravity, because without the need for redemption, the other points would be irrelevant.

The "U," then, stands for Unconditional Election. Election, or predestination as it is commonly called, is probably the most recognized of all five points. When someone hears the word "Calvinism," the first thing that usually comes to mind is predestination (and maybe a powerfully convicting delivery of Jonathon Edwards' sermon *Sinners in the Hands of an Angry God*.)

That's because all the points revolve around this one central truth. The Doctrines of Grace all seem to come back to this one concrete center point. Election is the foundation that Reformed Theology is built upon. And while it would take thousands of pages and countless hours to even scratch its surface, sufficed to say for our purposes here that it refers to God's choosing of us as opposed to our choosing of Him. Or as the Apostle Paul puts it in Roman 9:16, "It does not, therefore, depend of man's desire or effort, but on God's mercy." "For He says to Moses, 'I will have mercy on whom I have mercy, and I will have compassion on whom I have compassion'" (Romans 9:15).

If you haven't read through Romans 9 in its full context, I would strongly urge you to if you want a deeper understanding of election. A few other key passages are Ephesians 1 and 2, Colossians 3, Titus 3, 1 Peter 1, 1 Thessalonians 1, and 2 Thessalonians 2. But while Unconditional Election is the most recognizable of all five points, it is not the most controversial.

The third point, the "L," reserves that status, and it is—you guessed it—the one that four-point Calvinists reject. It stands for Limited Atonement, or the idea that while Christ's death on the cross was *sufficient* for all, it is only *efficient* for some. That is, Jesus' death and resurrection is powerful enough to save every person, but it only effectively saves the elect, whom God has called to salvation.

Of course, no Christian would argue that all people are saved. The question then becomes, does Jesus' death matter for those who reject Him and go to Hell? Five-point Calvinists argue that God's electing of some is no different than His dying for some. They contend that if Jesus died for everyone, then everyone would be saved.

It's not so simple for four-point Calvinists, though. They seem content with God choosing some and not others, but not with Him dying only for those who are chosen.

In Matthew 20:28, Jesus states His purpose of coming to earth to "serve, and to give his life as a ransom for many." The implication with the word *many* is *not all*. But a four-point Calvinist would interpret "many" to be all-inclusive, as if *many* is another way of saying *all*.

Despite what the word means, one thing is clear: Jesus' death, whether for all or only some, really matters only for those who accept Christ. Even if Jesus died for every person in existence, we know that the vast majority of the world will spend an eternity in Hell. This begs a crucial question—one that most Christians are scared to even confront: Does God love those people He sends to Hell for all eternity or not?

He has an awfully funny way of showing it if He does. The Bible describes Hell so vividly that no right-minded person would want to spend even one nanosecond there:

> But the subjects of the kingdom will be thrown outside, into the darkness, where there will be weeping and gnashing of teeth. (Matthew 8:12)

> Those who hate the LORD would cringe before Him, and their punishment would last forever. (Psalm 81:15)

> And the smoke of their torment rises for ever and ever. There is no rest day or night for those who worship the beast and his image, or for anyone who receives the mark of his name. (Revelation 14:11)

I don't know about you, but this doesn't exactly sound like a place where I would want to spend eternity. The souls of Hell live forever in exquisite torment. They do not endure the pain and flames of punishment for a day, a week, a month, a year, a decade, a century, or even a millennium. They endure horrific suffering FOREVER!

Furthermore, they will be forced to bow before God and confess that He is Lord without any chance of ever being forgiven and accepted into Heaven.

Every believer knows this, but most still insist that God loves everyone. In a debate between Pastors John Rankin and Fred Phelps, Pastor Rankin argued that "God loves those who reject Christ enough to let them choose Hell." After hearing this statement, I couldn't help but laugh at how ridiculous of a claim that is. No logically minded person who understands anything at all about the realities of Hell would ever make such an illogical claim.

But after speaking with another pastor, I wondered if there may be a hint of truth in the statement that God still loves them in spite of sending them to Hell for eternity. This Pastor used an analogy to communicate his beliefs regarding God's love.

"I love all the children in my church," he said. "But I don't love them the same way I love my own children. In the same way, God loves all people, but He loves His own people in a much deeper, more affectionate way."

This pastor defined love differently than I do in this chapter. My definition of love is eternal benevolence, while this pastor's definition is more what I would call common grace. God does love sinners while they are on earth if you define His love as common grace. By this definition, allowing sinners to breathe is a loving act on God's part. The love I am referring to, however, goes much deeper than that. It is an eternal benevolence that God graciously bestows upon His children. It is directed at the objects of His mercy and exists to demonstrate His glory through giving them matchless joy. By either definition, the souls in Hell do not experience God's love in any form because no benevolence or common grace exists for the souls in Hell.

In support of his position, the pastor also quoted Matthew 5:43-45, where Jesus commands us to love our enemies: "You have heard that it was said, 'Love your neighbor and hate your enemy.' But I tell you: Love your enemies and pray for those who persecute you, that you may be sons of your Father in heaven. He causes His sun to rise on the evil and the good, and sends rain on the righteous and the unrighteous."

Again, these verses in Matthew 5 reference God's love by its common grace definition. The sun and rain are gifts that the Lord graciously provides to all people, whether they belong to Him or not.

Still, Jesus Himself, who is God, commands us to love our enemies in this passage, so let's assume for the sake of argument that Jesus is defining His love here by the eternal benevolence definition. By that definition, it stands to reason that He too must love His enemies. Would He give us a command that He doesn't hold Himself accountable to?

Contrary to popular belief, God gives many commands that He does not hold Himself to. He commands us, for instance, to not be jealous, but in Exodus 20:3-5 and 34:14 God demands that we not worship other gods because He is a jealous God and is provoked to anger when worthless idols take His place. In both passages, God admits that He is the very thing He commands us to not be. The same thing is true in relation to pride. God commands us to not be prideful, saying in Proverbs 8:13, "I hate pride and arrogance." As the supreme ruler of the universe, however, God reserves the right to be prideful and to demand our eternal worship for the perfect deity that He is. Likewise, He commands us to not judge others, but He will ultimately judge everyone (2 Timothy 4:1, 1 Peter 4:5).

The real question, then, is: is Jesus' command to love our enemies indicative of God's nature, or is it a command, similar to those mentioned, that God does not hold Himself accountable to?

As I've demonstrated above, God is entitled to be certain things that He does not allow us, as His subjects, to be. But is being loving toward one's enemies one of those things?

Why does God command us to love our enemies? My guess is that by loving our enemies who are not yet saved, we are filled with a passion to lead them to Christ. Without love for our enemies, evangelism would not exist.

Unlike us, however, God already knows who will be saved. He has, in fact, determined who will be saved even before the foundation of the world. Is it necessary, then, for God to love His enemies?

As with any theological question, all we are left with is God's Word. When in doubt, turn to the Bible, and as a general rule the answers will be right there, saturating each page, ready and waiting to invade our minds.

So what does the Bible say?

We've touched on the nature of God's love, but so far we haven't evaluated His hatred. Most Christians refuse to acknowledge the hatred of God because it doesn't fit the modern image of a lenient, gentle deity who loves and accepts every human thought, choice, or action. Unfortunately, the God of the Bible is not at all the giant teddy bear many Christians make Him out to be.

He is, indeed, loving, but He is wrathful as well. He is wrathful enough to wipe out countless people in a devastating flood, to destroy Sodom and Gomorrah with fire and brimstone, to cause the earth to open up and swallow idolaters and wicked pagans, to exterminate Jericho and the Canaanites, and even to damn the souls of the unrighteous to Hell forever. Watch what David says about God's hatred in the Psalms:

> The arrogant cannot stand in your presence; *you hate all who do wrong.* (Psalm 5:5)

The LORD examines the righteous, but *the wicked and those who love violence his soul hates*. (Psalm 11:5).

You love righteousness and hate wickedness... (Psalm 45:7)

The One enthroned in heaven laughs; the Lord scoffs at them. Then He rebukes them in his anger and terrifies them in his wrath. (Psalm 2:4-5)

Then in Hosea 9:15, we read, "Because of all their wickedness in Gilgal, I *hated them* there. Because of their sinful deeds, I will drive them out of my house. *I will no longer love them;* all their leaders are rebellious."

Clearly God hates. And according to the above verses, He doesn't just hate the sins being committed, He also hates the people committing them. He hates "all who do wrong," according to Psalm 5:5 and "the wicked and those who love violence," according to Psalm 11:5. In Hosea 9:15, the Lord even testifies to taking His love from the wicked of Gilgal.

These powerful verses tell us two things: first, that God hates people who do wrong, and second, that He doesn't just hate some people who do wrong; He hates *all* who continually engage in wickedness.

Is this still true today, though? Does God's wrath still burn with the terrible dread it did thousands of years ago? After all, this image of a just, wrathful God is far removed from the modern images we've grown so accustomed to.

The answer to this fearful question is a resounding *YES*. God is exactly the same today as He was yesterday and as He will be tomorrow and for all eternity. Hebrews makes this abundantly clear. The author writes, "Jesus Christ is the same yesterday, today, and forever" (Hebrews 13:8).

Like His son, God the Father is constant. In Revelation 22:13 He declares, "I am the Alpha and the Omega, the First and the Last, the Beginning and the End." God is perfect, and perfection cannot change, because if it did it would no longer be perfect.

So God loves, and God hates. Can His love and hatred co-exist? Can the righteous judge of the universe love the wicked while simultaneously hating them? Is God's relationship to sinners a genuine "love-hate relationship?"

In the same debate I referenced earlier, Pastor Phelps made a very poignant comparison that struck a chord in me. He pointed out that just as a judge sends a criminal to prison, so too God sends the sinner to Hell. Separating the sinner from his sin, he points out, is just as impossible as separating the criminal from his crime.

"Who does the judge send to the penitentiary?" he asks. "The criminal, or the crime?"

"Who does God send to Hell? The sinner, or just his sin?"

"It is a metaphysical impossibility to separate the sin from the sinner."

No matter how tragically unbelievable his words may sound, Pastor Phelps is right. God does not separate the sin from the sinner. He sends the sinner to Hell along with his sins. God does not cast sins into eternal fire, He casts *sinners* into it. But does God still love the sinner?

To answer this question, it is imperative that we understand the nature of God's hatred. The hatred of God is not an evil passion as it is with men. God's attribute of hatred is not motivated by evil, vindictiveness, or spitefulness in any way. Rather, God's hatred is perfect (Psalm 139:22 KJV). It is a fixed determination, whereby God intentionally and righteously punishes the impenitent wicked forever in order to demonstrate His righteousness, justice, and glory.

Hatred is, indeed, an attribute of God, just as love is. Both exist in the Almighty, and He shows His love through the riches of His mercy in saving unworthy sinners and the power of His perfect hatred by justly damning the reprobate to eternal suffering.

In Malachi 1, the Lord discusses His attributes of hatred and love:

> "I have loved you," says the LORD. "But you ask, 'How have you loved us?'" "Was not Esau Jacob's brother?" the LORD says. "Yet I have loved Jacob, but Esau I have hated, and I have turned his mountains into a wasteland and left his inheritance to the desert jackals." (Malachi 1:2-3)

This passage is absolutely crucial to putting God's love and hatred into proper perspective. God's people ask Him how He has loved them. They ask very plainly, "How have you loved us?" In response, God states, "I have loved Jacob, but Esau I have hated." In this instance, God defines His love for His people by first defining His hate. He tells them that His love for them is proven by the fact that He chose to hate Esau but love Jacob and, thus, them.

Take note that in this passage God makes the riches of His grace wonderfully known. As the Lord reminds His people here, we understand God's love for us by first understanding His hatred and the fact that while we are worthy of receiving eternal punishment for our sins and the full extent of God's hatred and righteous judgment, He has lovingly saved us from damnation through Christ.

The same God who infinitely loves His elect, however, also perfectly hates the reprobate and exercises His perfect hatred in justly sending their souls to Hell for all eternity. God's attributes of love and hatred are both undeniable as we examine Scripture, and the notion that God loves the souls He sends to Hell to suffer exquisite torment forever is, quite frankly, absurd and illogical.

My conclusions are based on my definitions of God's love and hatred as they exist in the Bible. This chapter will, no doubt, be the most controversial of this entire book, but understanding as much as possible about God's nature is vital to spiritual growth and is only possible when terms are placed in their appropriate contexts.

As you plunge deeper into this difficult question, keep in mind that God is God. He is perfect, righteous, just, and infinitely holy. Everyone and everything (including those He sends to Hell) exists solely for His glory, and as Paul reminds us in Romans 9, if God desires to make some vessels for honorable use and others for destruction, He is perfectly entitled to do so.

Hatred is unavoidably a characteristic of God in Scripture, but what do *you* make of it? As for me, I will say that based on Scripture, logic, and everything I know about God's love and hatred, I am certain that God does not love the reprobate. More specifically, I am certain that God does not love them with the love of eternal benevolence with which He loves His elect. By the common grace definition of love, God does, in a sense, love the reprobate while they are on earth, but not after they enter damnation, as no more grace exists for them in Hell. By either definition of love, the love of God does not exist in any way, shape, or form for the souls suffering in Hell, and according to the definitions of God's love and hatred that I have set forth, this conclusion is inarguable.

Regardless of whether God loves the reprobate in any sense or not, the common assumption that God "hates the sin but loves the sinner" is all but clear in the Bible. It is yet another misconception that should be given careful consideration and evaluated in its full context before adding it to one's list of common sayings. The idea that God does not love all people in no way diminishes His love for *His* people, though, and that is a very comforting reality for believers. It should also motivate us to reach the lost so they may avoid the torments of God's hatred and experience His infinite, unfailing love.

Despite what your current beliefs are, I would encourage you to search your heart, study further, narrowly define your terms, and use caution when you proclaim that God "hates the sin but loves the sinner."

Questions for Reflection

1. What do you think? Does God hate sinners or just their sins? Keep in mind the term *sinner* is referring to unbelievers who are slaves to sin, not saved people, though they too still struggle with sin.

2. How do you view God's attributes of love and hatred after reading this chapter?

3. As a believer, do you feel any different knowing that God's love may be reserved solely for you and other Christians? Do you feel more loved or merely confused?

4 | *"Free Will"*

As you read the first chapter of this book, you may have found yourself wondering exactly which of my friend Tom's hot topics got me so fired up. I mentioned that Calvinism was the dominant theme of our conversation, but I neglected to mention the specific tenet of Calvinism we spent most of our time hashing out.

The comment Tom made that I was completely unwilling to accept is that man has no free will when it comes to his salvation.

What kind of heretic could believe such a thing? I thought. Every Christian knows that God gives us the free will to either choose Him or reject Him. It's our choice. God freely offers salvation to everyone, and it's the job of each individual to accept that free gift.

Or so I thought.

The above statement is true to a point. If by *will* we mean the ability of humans to choose to act on their strongest desires, then I would never argue against the notion that man has free will. As we saw in the previous chapter, defining terms becomes very important. The will of man, however, is limited in that man's will to choose Christ—for the Lord to be his strongest desire—is not uninhibited. Men are only capable of freely choosing Christ when God supernaturally draws them to His son and graciously enables men to make the choice they make. In this sense, the will of man is not truly free in relation to salvation.

You see, like most of the myths in this book, the myth of free will is partially true, but not entirely true. The question Reformed Theology raises is not whether man has the free will to accept Christ, but rather whether he is entirely free, or uninhibited, in making that choice. In other words, the question is really *who* gives man the insight to make the choice he makes. Does man, of his own wisdom—a wisdom which according to 1 Corinthians 3:19 is "foolishness in God's sight"—possess the ability or even the desire to choose Christ? 1 Corinthians 1:18 calls the message of the cross "foolishness to those who are perishing." If you recall from Chapter 2, Romans 3 also paints a clear picture of man's innate wickedness and inability to "seek" God.

We know, then, that God must be the initiator of our redemption. Because of our tragic inability to even desire to seek Him, God Himself must quicken our hearts before a change can occur in us. In John 6:44, Jesus states, "No one can come to me unless the Father who sent me draws him."

It doesn't get much clearer than that. Jesus makes it crystal clear that *no man* can come to Him (or be saved) without first being drawn by the Father. The choice then is only "free" in so much as God allows us to freely make it. That is, without God's initiation in drawing us to Christ and allowing us to freely choose Him, we would have no freedom to choose Christ on our own because Jesus would never be our strongest desire.

But if we have no freedom in our choice apart from God, how can God blame us when we do not choose Christ? How can He hold us accountable for not accepting Him when He has to drive us to that acceptance in the first place?

Paul addresses this same question (or accusation, really) in Romans 9:

> One of you will say to me: 'Then why does God still blame us? For who resists His will?' But who are you, O man, to talk back to God?
> Shall what is formed say to him who formed it, 'Why did you make me like this?' Does not the potter have the right to make out of the same lump of clay some pottery for noble purposes and some for common use? What if God, choosing to show his wrath and make his power known, bore with great patience the objects of his wrath—prepared for destruction? What if he did this to make the riches of his glory known to the objects of his mercy, whom he prepared in advance for glory— even us, whom he has called, not only from the Jews but also from the Gentiles? (Romans 9:19-24)

The above passage is one of the most awesome reminders of God's sovereignty in the entire Bible. Paul's words evoke the reality that we are nothing compared to God. We are finite, sinful, mortal, insignificant, feeble-minded human beings who stand in sharp contrast to the awesome power and majesty of our Maker. As the mere creations of our Master's hand, we are unworthy of questioning God's sovereignty in our lives. He is our Master, we are His subjects. He is the potter, we are the clay. He calls the shots, we simply obey. We live for His glory, He does not live for ours.

For God to hold those who do not accept Jesus accountable, however, a certain degree of freedom has to exist. If man had no freedom at all, God could not hold him responsible; for no one can be punished for something they are incapable of committing.

John Calvin says it very well in *Bondage and Liberation of the will:*

> We allow that man has choice and that it is self-determined, so that if he does anything evil, it should be imputed to him and to his own voluntary choosing. We do away with coercion and force, because this contradicts the nature of the will and cannot coexist with it. We deny that choice is free, because through man's innate wickedness it is of necessity driven to what is evil and cannot seek anything but evil. And from this it is possible to deduce what a great difference there is between necessity and coercion. For we do not say that man is dragged unwillingly into sinning, but that because his will is corrupt he is held captive under the yoke of sin and therefore of necessity will in an evil way. For where there is bondage, there is necessity. But it makes a great difference whether the bondage is voluntary or coerced. We locate the necessity to sin precisely in corruption of the will, from which follows that it is self-determined.

To have a will, as Calvin points out, is to have a freedom of choice. When we say a person *wills,* we mean he makes a choice. That is precisely what it means to have a will. Jonathan Edwards defines the will more specifically as "the mind choosing." Man is free to choose what he desires, and the greatest of his desires will always be his winning choice. Walter J. Chantry writes, "Every man has the ability to choose his own words, to decide what his actions will be. We have a faculty of self-determination in the sense that we select our own thoughts, words, and deeds. Man is free to choose what he prefers, what he desires."

He is not free, however, in a larger sense. While man retains a certain degree of self-determination, God maintains control over man's final outcome. At this very moment, you have many choices. You may elect to stop reading this book, to take a nap, to eat, to sing, to walk, to continue reading, or to do anything else you prefer that is within your power. Whichever of these choices is your strongest desire (if any) will be what you ultimately decide to do. But one thing you are not capable of, apart from God, is choosing Christ. Without God's supernatural draw to Christ through the Holy Spirit, your greatest desire—your mind's choosing, in Edwards' words— will never be Christ.

Martin Luther went so far as to say, "If any man doth ascribe of salvation, even the very least, to the free will of man, he knoweth nothing of grace, and he hath not learnt Jesus Christ aright." A simpler version of Luther's quote is "If anyone says man's free will has anything to do with salvation, he misunderstands the meaning of grace and has a warped perception of Jesus."

Luther's insistence here is rooted in the fundamental truth that all glory is due God for every good outcome, including salvation. Grace is God's willingness to freely give us what we don't deserve and to forgive us when we don't deserve to be forgiven, for no other reason than the kind intention of His will. If we as human beings are responsible for any part of our salvation and can claim credit for our part, then glory is stolen from God and part of His credit is transferred to us.

This, of course, can never happen. As John the Baptist declares in John 3:30, "He must become greater; I must become less." Like John, our aim should be to glorify God and abase man. He must become more as we become less. We must be humbled, He must be magnified.

To Christians concerned with God's complete glorification, the argument against free will is not merely a logical one, it is downright common sense. But beyond the logic is the more important fact that the term "free will" is foreign to God's Word in all its translations.

Free will as a phrase does not appear in the Bible. The two words never once appear side by side in any translation. Yet this phrase has been abused more than almost any other throughout the history of Christendom. Churches incorporate the phrase into their names, like "Free Will Baptist Church" or "Free Will Assembly of God." Congregations sing of free will during contemporary worship services. Christians have bought into the myth of free will more than perhaps any other modern misconception.

A term or concept is not necessarily invalid just because it doesn't appear in the Bible, though. Many widely accepted theological principles do not exist verbatim in the Bible, but that does not render them false. The word *trinity,* for instance, is not in the Bible. It is an entirely man-made term, developed by scholars to recognize the godhead, or the triune nature of God. I will not challenge the concept of the trinity, although it is not a part of the Bible, because I believe in its validity.

Scripture gives equal weight to all three entities of the trinity—especially in terms of their work in salvation. God the Father draw us to the son, the son's death and resurrection justify us and allow us entrance into paradise, and the Holy Spirit quickens our hearts to faith, obedience, and maturity in Christ. Without any one of these parts, salvation cannot occur. The trinity may not be mentioned in the Bible, but it is just as credible as if it were.

I wish that were true for more modern misconceptions, but it is not true for most. Like the trinity, free will is nowhere to be found, but unlike the trinity, free will is an ambiguous concept. I don't mean to say that the trinity isn't difficult to understand—it is probably one of the *most* difficult concepts to fathom in our faith; but the notion of free will raises more doubt and calls more into question.

If you've been a card carrying member of the "free will club" for any length of time, chances are you're probably experiencing the same feelings of anger, frustration, and confusion that I did years ago. The free will debate has raged for centuries, ever since Saint Augustine first debated over the issue with Pelagius in the early fifth century, and probably before then.

We will not answer the question over how far free will's reach extends, but we can certainly unravel more behind its mystery. One thing's for sure: if my free will is powerful enough to save me, then I am doomed from my first breath and God is not worthy of praise. Indeed, God has limited my will and taken control of my life's reigns so that I may have life. He has freely willed to bestow His matchless grace upon me. I am an object of mercy, not a vessel for destruction, because God has planned my choice in Him before the beginning of time. I am free because He has denied me my complete freedom. For that, I thank God.

Questions for Reflection

1. Before reading this chapter, how would you have defined "free will?" How would you define the meaning of it now?

2. Aside from God's supernatural draw in your life, do you think you could choose Him on your own? Could you even desire to?

3. Does knowing that God controls your choice in Him frustrate you or give you peaceful reassurance?

4. Have you made a habit of crediting God or yourself with your salvation? Who will you credit now?

5 | "The Bible Is a Good Set of Guidelines, but It Isn't Perfect"

My first response to people when I hear them make the heretical claim that the Bible is merely a set of good principles to live by is a question. I ask how it is that they can profess to believe in an omniscient, omnipotent God and then doubt His ability to perfectly inspire His Word.

Ironically enough, the Bible is the only source of knowledge we have of God, aside from creation itself, so the above statement is flawed from the beginning. All the knowledge we glean about God comes from His Word and His Word alone. How can we believe one thing the Bible says (in this case God's infinite power), but reject other portions of it?

Let's travel back in time for a moment to our discussion about the different sects within modern Christianity. Do you remember the four groups?

The first group (the devout group) would never doubt any portion of God's Word. They base their understanding on Scripture alone, or *Sola Scriptura,* as we reformers call it. The second group would not likely challenge the supremacy of the Bible, either, because they would be too afraid to. But many members of the last two groups would challenge the Bible's authority and often disregard entire portions of it.

The beef the doubters have with the Bible is that it was written by men. The notion that God divinely inspired the authors of His Word to perfectly communicate all He wants the world to know is too far fetched for them.

I find it amazing that the idea that God worked through the pens of men is any more unbelievable to some than His pure existence. Of course if God exists and is as powerful as the Bible describes Him, communicating His Word flawlessly through men was all but challenging for Him. In fact, compared to the other miracles we read about, that one is relatively minor. Inspiring a few decrepit old men to write perfect text is nothing compared to creating the universe, raising Lazarus from the dead, feeding five thousand, giving sight to the blind, or making a lame man rise and walk. If Jesus was able to accomplish all that, inspiring the Bible is a miracle fit for His vacation.

Speaking to the Thessalonians, Paul said, "And we also thank God continually because, when you received the word of God, which you heard from us, you accepted it not as the word of men, but as it actually is, the word of God, which is at work in you who believe" (1 Thessalonians 2:13). He then informs us in 2 Timothy 3:16 that "all Scripture is God-breathed and is useful for teaching, rebuking, correcting and training in righteousness."

Not *some* Scripture—a*ll* Scripture is God-breathed and is useful in a number of ways. The Bible is not an owner's manual on life, stuffed in a glove box, collecting dust, waiting to be pulled out only in the midst of a crisis.

Unfortunately, many professing Christians view it as just that. They see the Bible as a set of moral instructions that come in handy from time to time but hold no real bearing in life. They pay close attention to select sections they agree with but dismiss the rest like an old dishrag. The portions they agree with are the ones they deem "God-breathed," while the remaining hundreds of pages are the useless scribbles of a few mortal men in their eyes.

Other authors argue vehemently for the inerrancy of the Bible. In the fall of 1978, roughly three hundred noted evangelical scholars attended an international Summit Conference at the Hyatt Regency O'Hare in Chicago and produced the "Chicago Statement on Biblical Inerrancy." R. C. Sproul, who participated in the conference and signed the statement, wrote an official commentary on the articles titled *Explaining Inerrancy.* In it, he systematically defends and proves Biblical inerrancy. His argument is so concrete that no reasonably minded person could refute it, and I recommend reading it if you wish to learn more about this topic.

The word *inerrant* means "infallible"—free from error. To be inerrant is to be perfect, so when you see the term *Biblical Inerrancy,* it is referring to the perfect essence of the Bible. Nothing is in the Bible that shouldn't be, and nothing is left out that should be in it.

The idea that any book is absolutely flawless is ridiculous to most people—even the Bible, although it is of an entirely different nature and is widely regarded as a holy book. Many versions have "The Holy Bible" etched right into their leather covers. Before we so much as open our Bibles, we are reminded of their holy status. We are filled with a sense that the words we are about to read are not the mere ramblings of a sinful human being, but the perfect imperatives of the Most High God.

To be *holy* is to be set apart. So, while the Bible is a book of ink, pages, and binding like any other, it is very different from all other books in its holiness, or otherness. It is set apart from them because it is the only holy book in existence. Just as we are depraved and separate from God, the books of this world (including this one) are on an entirely different plain than the Bible. There is only one Word of God, and that Word reigns supreme above all others.

We refer to the Bible as the "Word" of God. But have you ever wondered why? Have you paid close attention to that phrase? Has anything struck you a bit odd about referring to the Bible in that way?

The Bible is made up of many words just like any other book, so why, you might ask, do we call it the "Word" (singular) of God instead of the "words" of God, or the "revelation" of God, or even the "book" of God?

The reason is very simple: the Bible, with all its words, verses, passages, chapters, and books, collectively forms the entire Word of God. All its parts constitute its whole. That is, everything in the Bible combined together embodies the one complete version of God's revelation to man. And this is why the Bible is referred to as the "Word" of God—singular, not plural.

What an awesome display of power and glory. We read many instances of God displaying His glory through simplicity. When He commands His people, He often ends the command with "I am the Lord," as if to say, "This is not negotiable. What I say goes. Period." God instructed Moses to tell His people to call Him "I AM." Phrases like these are so simple, yet so profound. They are so powerful they can make the strongest men tremble and the proudest men fall to their knees in humility. I become so filled with a sense of awe and wonder when I encounter passages like these that I can't help but pause for a moment to bask in the glory and splendor of our awesome Lord.

Passages that evoke such awe are intimidating and are exactly the type that many readers stray away from. Our feeble minds can't begin to fathom a power so great that its possessor is capable of literally anything. Disbelieving readers find every reason to challenge the Bible's legitimacy as an error-free text, in part, because their fear drives them to. They grow so terrified at the words of the Lord that they attempt to discredit them in an effort to merely put themselves at ease.

One such attempt is evident in their insistence that the Bible was written by men, which we know is true in a physical sense because most of its many books were authored by different people at different times. This fact alone seems to be enough fuel for the doubters' fire, but they still find other excuses to challenge the Bible's supremacy.

Beyond the authors' pens, skeptics of Biblical inerrancy cite another factor that causes them to question the Bible's authority. In addition to men authoring the Bible, they have a hard time justifying why certain books were included as part of the canon while other books were rejected. A number of books were denied the right to be part of the Holy book. These books, collectively referred to as the *Apocrypha,* have questionable origins, but critics question whether they should have actually been allowed into the canon.

To address this question, I revert back to the same argument I posed over the Bible's authorship. If we believe that God is as powerful as the Bible portrays Him, it should not be beyond our scope of imagination to view Him as capable of not only inspiring the pens of men, but also their filtering and organizational skills. If God inspired the authors of His Word to write exactly what He wanted, He most assuredly inspired those who compiled it to include the books He intended to be included in the text and to exclude the books He wanted omitted. He would not start such an important project and simply leave it improperly unfinished.

To claim that portions of the Bible are flawed is to accuse God, who is perfect, of making mistakes. Anyone who knows anything about the God of the Bible knows this is one accusation to never dare make. We serve God because He is awesome—because He is beyond our comprehension. If He were in any way attainable to us, He would not be worth worshipping. And if the Bible were flawed in any way, God's perfection, power, and mystery would become null and void. In other words, if God were capable of making any mistake, including the mistake of allowing His own Word to be flawed, then He would not be perfect and would not be worthy of praise.

The truth is, anyone who truly believes in God believes in His awesome power and that His power was more than sufficient enough to divinely inspire every word of the Bible. For unbelievers, the inerrancy of scripture poses a threat because the Bible vividly depicts the wages of sin.

For Christians, the inerrancy of the Bible is a beacon of hope in a world of darkness. It is the rock we can always cling to as we seek to grow in our faith and a mighty weapon as we face our enemies in defense of our beliefs. As Christians, every claim we make should be backed by Scripture. We should check everything we hear to ensure that it is, in fact, in the Bible and accurate in the context in which it is presented. This is precisely why we all open our Bibles and read along in church, and the lack of this examination is exactly why misconceptions like the ones addressed in this book arise.

Spiritual growth requires careful study of Scripture, and the only way to give the Bible its due attention is to read it without ceasing, giving careful consideration to each word, verse, and passage. Often times this means referring to the original Greek or Hebrew.

The Old Testament was originally written in Hebrew, while the New Testament was written in Greek, and the challenge with both languages is that they commonly use numerous words to express the same concept in a variety of ways. For instance, the Greek words *agape*, *philia*, and *eros* are all translated into English as the word "love." All three words connote very different meanings, however. *Eros* is indicative of a sexual or physical kind of love, while *philia* refers to a brotherly, fraternal type of love. Contrary to both, *agape* love expresses a much deeper love—a divine, sacrificial love that is volitional and thoughtful. Jesus demonstrates the significance of each term in a discussion with Simon Peter:

> When they had finished eating, Jesus said to Simon Peter, "Simon son of John, do you truly love (*eros)* me more than these?" "Yes, Lord," he said, "you know that I love you." Jesus said, "Feed my lambs." Again Jesus said, "Simon son of John, do you truly love (*philia)* me?" He answered, "Yes, Lord, you know that I love you." Jesus said, "Take care of my sheep." The third time he said to him, "Simon son of John, do you love (*agape)* me?" Peter was hurt because Jesus asked him the third time, "Do you love me?" He said, 'Lord, you know all things; you know that I love you." Jesus said, "Feed my sheep." (John 21:15-17)

The first two times, Jesus questions Peter's love for Him as a brother or friend. He uses the Greek *eros* and *philia* to elicit a certain response from Peter. The third and last time he questions Peter, He calls into question Peter's love for Him on a much greater scale. He asks Peter if he truly loves Him not only as a close friend and teacher, but as his Master, his Savior and Redeemer. This *agape* love is entirely different than the other two forms Jesus addresses, and He intentionally distinguishes between all three in His interaction with Peter. Thus, it is imperative to know their differences.

Passages like this one demonstrate the crucial importance of studying Scripture in a disciplined, thorough manner. A false understanding of the above passage would cause one to believe that Jesus was simply being redundant in questioning Peter and irritating him to the point of unbearable frustration. By thoroughly analyzing the text, however, we find that Jesus was revealing the importance of divine love through Simon Peter.

In this particular scenario, the original text had to be researched for the meaning of the passage to be fully understood, but in many cases a thorough reading of Scripture requires nothing more than a willingness to simply read slowly, think critically, or discuss the passage with a close friend. Praying about your biblical studies is, of course, the most important habit to adopt, as a strong prayer life will open your heart and mind to wisdom and accurate interpretation of God's Word.

The bottom line is this: to believe in God is to believe in the Bible. Without the Bible, we have no knowledge of God to begin with, and any choosing on man's part as to what parts to believe or dismiss is not only futile, it's grossly arrogant. If a person believes in the God of the Bible, she must believe in His power. And if she believes in His power, she must acknowledge His power in divinely inspiring His holy Word. Why would such an awesome God allow His perfection to be tainted? *How* could He allow it? He can't, because He is perfect and He *never* makes mistakes. So, the next time you sit down to read your Bible, think of what you've learned from reading this chapter and rest assured that every word you read has been breathed straight from the mouth of the one living God.

Questions for Reflection

1. Do you believe that the Bible is truly inerrant in spite of the fact that it was written by men? Although men physically authored the Bible, did they *truly* author it or did God?

2. How much emphasis do you put on Scripture as a driving force in your spiritual growth? Do you rely on it fully or partially? How heavily will you rely on it now?

3. Is there any better tool you can think of to defend your Christian beliefs than the very Word of God itself?

6 | *"It's Not a Religion, It's a Relationship"*

I remember driving in my car as a teenager, spending countless hours listening to a Christian radio station called Radio U. My friends and I loved Radio U because the music was very contemporary and seemed to fly in the face of more traditional stations that we thought were boring. The station's catch slogan, which was played between nearly every song, was, "Radio U: where it's not a religion, it's a relationship."

As a kid, I thought the catch phrase was cool—a new age rebellion that sought to challenge the established religious system and break down the barriers of intimidating imposition. But as an adult, wiser and more experienced, I find this statement more ridiculous than insightful.

The goal of Christian radio stations, books, magazines, television networks, and other media outlets is to attract as many listeners or viewers as possible, and they assume that the greatest way to do so is to create a sense of a contemporary church culture that appeals to people today. The antiquated view of stained glass windows, stone pillars, burning candles, and ironclad lanterns creates a grossly unappealing view of the church in an age where fashion and modernity run rampant. Pews are replaced with padded chairs, fellowship halls are converted into multi-purpose gymnasiums, and giant movie screens occupy the spaces where hymn boards were once nailed to the wall.

None of these changes are innately evil, but the attempt to separate religion from the Christian faith is an act that goes beyond a few changes with the times.

Merriam-Webster's Dictionary defines religion as "the service and worship of God or the supernatural," "commitment or devotion to religious faith or observance," or "a cause, principle, or system of beliefs held to with ardor and faith."

Do you, as a Christian, serve and worship God? Are you committed and devoted to your faith? Do you hold to your system of beliefs with ardor and faith?

If you answered "yes" to these questions, then by definition you are religious. And by calling yourself a Christian, you confess to your participation in the Christian religion.

Like the old hymn board and gaudy lanterns, the word *religion* seems too archaic for modern times. That's exactly why the phrase "it's not a religion, it's a relationship" came into existence. The term "relationship" is much less intimidating and fits better with the romantic paradigm of our faith. By focusing on the relationship alone, it seems as though Christ is a friend, a buddy who we can talk with and whose shoulder we can cry on in hard times. He is that, but He is much more than that. He is our Lord and Savior, our Redeemer and friend.

My barber recently told me that her husband decided to search for a new church because their pastor was so caught up in banning the word "religious" from their congregation. She said her husband became very upset when he was going over a passage with the youth group and the pastor told the kids to tell him to "stop being religious."

Those who emphasize the relational aspect of religion and disregard the term *religion* are committing a grievous error. I have had countless discussions with close friends who adamantly insist that one's relationship with Christ is all that matters and doctrinal issues are nothing but stumbling blocks that divide churches.

Doctrine, though, is the substance of any church. Without a concrete set of beliefs, a relationship with Christ cannot exist. A Christian's entire belief system is built on doctrine, and those beliefs influence all that one does. As a Calvinist, my relationship with Christ is vastly different than an Arminian brother's because we see God and the Gospel in entirely different ways. My doctrine causes me to see God as my sovereign Master who has chosen me in His mercy to partake in the riches of His glory forever. An Arminian's doctrine forces him to see God as one whose power is partially limited and whose goal is to grant everyone entrance into heaven.

Yes, a believer's relationship with God is of crucial importance, but what enhances that relationship? What ignites its flame in the first place?

Before a relationship with God can even occur, you must first understand what it means to accept Christ. And in order to understand, you have to know doctrine. That is, to understand God and your salvation, you must first understand religion because religion, or a set of beliefs, is how you learn anything about God and what it means to be saved.

To know God is to know doctrine. To be a Christian is to be religious. There is simply no way around it.

When I go through this chain of logic with other Christians, most of them concede the point. They admit that as Christians they are inevitably religious, but they go on to confess their dislike for the word itself. The mere word "religious" rubs them the wrong way because of all the negative images it connotes.

Many of them simply try to replace the word with another that sits better with them. Members of the fourth group of Christians do just that by replacing the word "religious" with the word "spiritual" because "spiritual" sounds better and connotes more pleasing images for them.

Being "spiritual," however, is not at all the same as being "religious." Spirituality relates to the intangible, or immaterial nature of the soul. Anyone who recognizes the soul as a mysterious and real part of their being is spiritual. To be religious, on the other hand, is to practice a particular religion, to embrace a set of beliefs in relation to the divine. There is certainly a religious component ingrained within spirituality, but religion is only one of many elements that constitute the whole meaning of the word. Spirituality is primarily concerned with discovering one's true nature or identity as it relates to the rest of creation and life.

Religion takes spirituality a step further and focuses on a believer's spiritual relationship with Christ and how that internal change affects man's relationship with the rest of the world once he is saved. To be spiritual is to recognize that there is more to our lives than what we merely see; to be religious is to take that recognition and apply it to our relationship with the Lord. In other words, spirituality leads to religion, and religion leads to a relationship.

Having a relationship with God requires an understanding and acceptance of the free gift of salvation, which comes about when a believer devotes himself to the practice of faith, which we call religion. To be religious, he must first recognize that there is more to life than what he readily sees, and this realization is the essence of spirituality. This order of events does not change. Spirituality comes first, followed by religion, and then the relationship.

Any relationship fits this model. Let's examine a married couple and how each event occurs as their relationship develops. When the couple first meets, they are attracted to something beyond their ability to explain. They may be physically attracted to each other, or they may possess an aura that neither can help but be attracted to. The feelings they have are not based in anything concrete because at first they don't even know each other. They simply recognize that there may be something about each other that they would like to explore further. After a few dates, they begin to learn more about each other and begin to understand one another better. They learn each other's likes and dislikes, strengths and weaknesses, subtleties and nuances. After a while of learning about each other, they come to the realization that they are meant to be together, and not by chance, but by ordination of God, so they commit themselves to one another in a marital covenant with God to be one for the rest of their lives on earth and throughout eternity.

Do you see how the married couple's relationship evolves? They begin by not knowing each other, but recognizing that there's a hidden element—something mysterious that draws them to each other and makes them believe that there may be more to what they initially see or feel. Upon exploring their curiosities further, they learn more about each other, and that knowledge and understanding leads to an unbreakable commitment, consecrated by God and meant to last for all eternity.

The couple's initial attraction is comparable to a believer's initial state of spirituality. The believer feels as though there must be something more to life than being born, living, and dying, but isn't exactly sure what that extra element is. Upon searching for an answer as the couple does, he begins to unravel more of the mystery and ultimately finds his identity in Christ. He becomes religious as he grows in his faith and begins his walk with the Lord. Finally, just as the couple gets married to consecrate their commitment to one another, the believer unites with Christ as he accepts Jesus and vows to faithfully serve and obey Him. The moment of salvation can occur at any point along the way, but the believer must understand what it means to be saved before he can truly be saved.

Think about how you came to accept Christ. Did anything happen before you did? You obviously heard and understood the Gospel, and before that you knew that there must be more to life than what you already knew and understood. Now, as a born again Christian, you have a relationship with the Lord, and this relationship is very real. You communicate with God in prayer, you learn about Him through reading His Word, and you serve Him faithfully as He has called you to as His obedient son or daughter. But though you wouldn't deny having a relationship with God, would you call yourself religious?

Whether you would or not, if you are a practicing follower of Christ, you *are* religious and Christianity is your religion. Your relationship with God is hopefully a strong one, but for that relationship to exist at all and for you to continue to mature in your faith, you must be faithful to your religious beliefs and practices.

Being called religious only sounds bad because of what the term now signifies. But it is just that—a term, a label, an adjective to describe one's loyalty to a divine set of beliefs. What's really important is what the word stands for, not what it connotes in the contemporary church setting. If you are a Christian, you are religious, and your religious doctrine shapes your understanding of God, and that understanding strengthens your relationship with Him. Be proud of your religion and the fact that as a son of God you are religious. And proudly proclaim to those who suggest otherwise, that Christianity "is both a religion and a relationship."

Questions for Reflection

1. Are you intimidated by the word "religion?" Have you tried to replace it with other terms that sound more appealing or less archaic to you?

2. Do you feel your relationship with God could even exist without first understanding doctrine and engaging in the religion of Christianity?

3. Accepting Christ is ultimately all that determines your salvation, but what causes your spiritual growth? Is simply believing enough to cause you to be as mature as you can be, or do you need to learn all you can through doctrine to obtain the greatest understanding of the Lord?

7 | *"Jesus Is My Copilot"*

The first time I saw a "Jesus is my copilot" bumper sticker, I thought nothing of it. I respected the driver who had the courage to unashamedly brand her car with a statement of her faith and hoped her display of boldness would encourage other Christians to follow her lead.

While I still respect that woman's willingness to unashamedly profess her faith in Christ, I realize now that the bumper sticker she flaunted, though admirable, was flawed.

"Jesus is my copilot" sends the wrong message to unbelievers. The catchy slogan may look great on the back of a sporty car, but the message it sends is not so flashy. This is because calling Jesus your copilot is really another way of calling Him your equal.

Copilots guide an aircraft together, and often times the copilot is the relief pilot, or the second in command. The root *co* means "together," so when it is used in a word, it signifies that the noun or verb the root is attached to is engaged in a cooperative act with someone or something else. A *co*ed dormitory, for instance, is one that houses both males and females. When two things "*co*exist," they exist together at the same time. To "*co*operate" is to work together toward a common goal, and to "*co*ordinate" is to place things together in the same order or class. These are just a few of hundreds of examples in which the root *co* signifies a togetherness and equality of at least two things.

Calling Jesus a copilot, then, is the symbolic equivalent of calling Him an equal. The metaphor has a two-fold meaning: it acknowledges Jesus as the copilot of the car that the person is driving, and on a deeper level it acknowledges His role as a guiding force in the person's life, as if to say that Jesus has hold of one of the reigns and is cooperatively steering the believer along the proper path.

Now, I'm fully aware that something as simple as a bumper sticker may not be of such a crucial nature that it necessitates a nit-picky dispute. After all, the other topics we've dealt with to this point have been pretty controversial and maybe even a little hard to take in. But understanding the truth behind this slogan is still quite important for the truth-seeking Christian. Recognizing God as the pilot of our lives and ourselves as mere passengers along for the ride creates an entirely new perspective on God's sovereignty and our humanity.

God is not our copilot, He is our pilot. He is the pilot of our plane, the driver of our car, the captain of our ship, and the coachman of our carriage. He takes the wheel, and we sit back for the ride, trusting that He will lead us as He sees fit and that He will fully accomplish His will in our lives.

When you read the slogan "Jesus is my copilot," what kind of scene comes to mind? If you're like me, you picture yourself seated in the cockpit of a small plane, beside Jesus, wearing oversized earphones and goggles, giving thumbs up to each other right before a thrilling, heart pounding takeoff.

Perhaps part of this ridiculous scene for me comes from a t-shirt I saw that said "Jesus is my copilot" with a picture of Jesus, just as I described Him, thumbs up and all.

This image of Jesus may be a bit comical at first glance, but I have to admit it disturbed me after my initial shock from seeing it dissipated. My convictions set in, and I felt guilty for even smirking at the disrespectful mockery pictured in front of me.

A girl I have known for years was wearing a similar shirt when I ran into her a couple years ago. Instead of saying "Jesus is my copilot," hers said "Jesus is my homeboy." Interestingly, this girl is a professing Christian, so I was especially appalled that she would dare to even purchase such a mocking, disrespectful shirt, let alone wear one for everyone to see.

Still, I tried to assume that making a mockery of her Savior was not her intent. I hoped that her goal with wearing the shirt was to appeal to unbelievers who may be more enticed by a humorous, albeit disrespectful, image of Christ.

My assumptions were shot down, though, when I encountered a group of high school age kids at a local mall wearing the same shirt. They were walking out of a gothic clothing store sporting purple, pink, and green hair, black lipstick, metal spikes, and long black trench coats. The rest of their attire was blatantly offensive and downright inappropriate for a public setting. Their shirts said "Jesus is my homeboy," but the rest of their clothing was stitched with pentagrams, swear words, and other satanic symbols.

I have no doubt that my acquaintance's motives were very opposite those of the kids I saw at the mall, but the fact that she was wearing the same shirt sends up a glaring red flag. If the haters of Christ wear a shirt in an effort to make a mockery of Jesus, chances are that shirt is not appropriate for a Christian to wear. Had it not been for the vile language that lined every other inch of their clothing, the girl I know would have appeared no different from them.

Jesus is not your homeboy and He is not your copilot, but let's see what the Bible calls Jesus to gain a better perspective on what we should hail Him as:

> And he will be called Wonderful Counselor, Mighty God, Everlasting Father, Prince of Peace. (Isaiah 9:6)

As we read, Jesus' title is one of grandeur. Every title named in Isaiah 9 is a royal title that evokes the awesome, immortal, and powerful supremacy of Christ as Lord and King over all. He is "wonderful," "mighty," "everlasting," and "peaceful." He is a "counselor," "father," "prince," and "God."

How would one of these titles fair on a t-shirt? They send a very different message than the others I've mentioned, don't they?

The WWJD bracelets, which seemed to go out of style a couple years ago, were admirable expressions of faith for those who wore them. The bracelets were simple, but they carried a powerful message. They acted as a constant daily reminder to ask oneself, "What would Jesus do?" in a given situation, and because virtually everyone was aware of the trend, even those who didn't wear bracelets would find themselves asking the question when they would see it on someone else's wrist.

The bracelets, unlike the "Jesus is my copilot" bumper sticker or the "Jesus is my homeboy" t-shirt, acknowledged God's supremacy. While the bumper sticker and shirt label Jesus as an equal, the bracelets depicted God as the leader, in that *His* actions, or "what Jesus would do," should determine *our* actions. That is, the bracelets forced us to think about Jesus as an authoritative, decisive figure whose perfect actions are far better than our own, while the bumper sticker and t-shirt make us view Christ as a co-decider along with us. Put more simply, the WWJD slogan acknowledged that Jesus' ways are better than our own and that His life is a model we should strive to emulate.

The WWJD bracelets put God in the pilot seat, but they seemed to run out of gas a few years back. A more recent display of God-centered humility is Carrie Underwood's hit single "Jesus, Take the Wheel." If you've heard this song, you are at least familiar with the chorus and may even have it memorized. In case you don't, the lyrics are as follows:

"Jesus, take the wheel
Take it from my hands
Cause I can't do this on my own
I'm letting go
So give me one more chance
To save me from this road I'm on
Jesus, take the wheel."

What I appreciate about this chorus is that it is really a prayer. It is directed at Jesus and, contrary to the "Jesus is my copilot" bumper sticker, it relinquishes all human effort over to God's power and direction. The believer who calls Jesus her copilot is saying, "Jesus, take *part of* the wheel; take it *along with* my hands. Cause I *can* do this on my own (but could use a little help to make sure I don't crash)."

I have no idea whether Carrie Underwood is a Christian or if she just made a hit single out of a song that a few other people composed, but the lyrics are what matter. Additionally, as a

Grammy winning single, awarded Best Country Song and maintaining the number one spot on the Billboard Country Singles chart for six weeks straight, "Jesus, Take the Wheel" poured through the speakers of more stereos and televisions than perhaps any other song in the country for at least a month and a half. It's safe to say that the name Jesus was heard by millions, if not billions, of people over that time period, and the message it sent painted an appropriate image of Christ, as opposed to many modern attempts to do the same. The song is secular, also, so millions of non-Christians at least heard the name Jesus and learned of the importance of allowing Him to lead their lives.

Do you view Jesus as your copilot, or would you ask Him to take full control of your wheel? Do you think you have enough power and ability to determine the course of your life along with God, or would you rather Him take complete control and trust in His ability to steer your course better than your own? Would you rather see Jesus seated beside you helping you navigate, or in front of you guiding your path?

I, for one, would hate to see how fast I would crash and burn if I put as much faith in my own abilities to find my way as I do in God's. I am proud to say that God is my pilot and I am just another passenger whose safety lies in the hands of the Almighty. No matter what turbulence may shake my journey, I can feel safe in the arms of He who made me and leads my way.

David says it best in Psalm 23, the most commonly quoted passage regarding a believer's comfort and security in God. In this famous passage, David calls God his shepherd and remarks that even in the darkest and most dreadful of times he "will fear no evil," for God is with him and comforts him.

Do you feel as secure in the hands of the Lord as David? Are you confident that your shepherd will never let you go astray and will always protect you from danger? Do you trust Him to lead you "in paths of righteousness," as David did?

I have to admit that at times I become arrogant and try to rely on my own devices to carry me through trials. When I feel as though God is leading me in a direction I don't want to go, I begin to lose faith and in fearful weakness I attempt to take control. I try to move from the passenger seat into the cockpit beside God. I go right from "back seat driver" to captain of the ship.

Everyone is guilty of losing faith from time to time. And though they may not realize it, Christians who put bumper stickers on their cars that label Jesus as their "copilot" are inadvertently giving in to the same weakness.

If your vehicle's rear end is the resting place for a "Jesus is my copilot" bumper sticker, don't take it off the car after reading this chapter. Instead, take a big black sharpie marker, walk outside, and cross out the "co" in "copilot." Likewise, if you own a "Jesus is my homeboy" t-shirt, replace the word "homeboy" with the word "Savior," and delight in how much better it feels to wear a shirt that exalts Christ instead of making a mockery of Him. Then, donned in your updated shirt and a WWJD bracelet, hop into your car, pop in "Jesus, Take the Wheel," and cruise down the road as others read that Jesus is your pilot, the leader and shepherd of your life.

Questions for Reflection

1. Have you seen the slogan "Jesus is my copilot" or "Jesus is my homeboy?" Maybe this book is the fist time you've heard of either phrase. Either way, what did you think the first time you saw them?

2. Do you see anything wrong with referring to Jesus as a "copilot" or "homeboy?" Do these words seem disrespectful or inappropriate to you? Why?

3. Can you think of better titles to describe the Lord? If so, what? Does Isaiah 9:6 ring a bell?

8 | *"You Don't Need to Go to Church to Be a Good Christian"*

How many times have you neglected going to church and used the popular excuse that you don't need to go to church to be a good Christian? We're all guilty of this common sin and have probably hidden behind this shameful excuse more times than we would like to admit. Claiming that church is not a necessity in a Christian's life is a convenient copout for those who would rather stay home on the Lord's Day. But why do so many people hide behind this popular excuse?

Most professing Christians who avoid church life cite political reasons for their evasion. They say that the church as a whole has become corrupt and has shifted its attention away from God and toward money. They deem their prior churches "legalistic," which means they judge members according to a strict code or set of regulations instead of their adherence to the Gospel. If a member isn't at church one week, seven people are calling to find out why she wasn't there. If a mother works outside the home, the pastor's wife rebukes her on occasion for not being a stay at home mom and raising her children properly. If a family earns a lot of money, they are labeled materialistic and given the cold shoulder by other less fortunate members.

While all of these facts may be true in many of today's churches, they do not act as "get out of church free" cards for Christians who suffer from them. God commands us to attend church for a number of reasons, and it is our duty to obey His commands, in spite of how corrupt others may be. God holds *us* accountable for our decisions, not others.

The element of accountability is a very important one for all Christians and is the very thing most of us fear. When I decided to move my family to the church we now belong to, my wife was not supportive of my decision. She had a plethora of reasons for not wanting to make the transition from our old church family to our current one, but after hours of open discussion, she admitted that the higher level of accountability is what frightened her most about making the move.

This is because our previous church was quite large. Most of the members didn't know half of the others because there were simply too many people for everyone to know each other well. Contrarily, the members of our current church make it a point to fellowship with each other every week, so no absence goes unnoticed and everyone knows if and why a person isn't in attendance.

The high level of accountability in churches threatens the privacy of members who do not want to be held responsible for their commitment to God. Such people view the church as a group of individuals, not the collective body of Christ. To them, church is a weekly meeting of acquaintances instead of an opportunity to fellowship with their Christian family and to learn about the Lord.

God's intention from the beginning has been for His

children to congregate as the church. The word "church," though, does not mean a building as Christ first uses the word in the New Testament.

Jesus first introduces the term in Matthew 16:18 when He tells Peter, "On this rock I will build my church, and the gates of Hades will not overcome it." The word *church,* as Christ used it, meant a body of believers. The church is the collective body of Christ—His bride as it is personified in Ephesians 5:25 when Paul instructs husbands to love their wives "just as Christ loved the church and gave Himself up for 'her.'" Attending church does not necessarily mean coming together under a steeple, sitting in pews, reading collectively from a pre-printed bulletin. As Jesus first described His church to Peter and the disciples, any meeting of believers is an act of participation in the church.

Paul refers to the church as a "household." In Ephesians 2:19, he writes, "Consequently, you are no longer foreigners and aliens, but fellow citizens with God's people and members of God's household." Again, in 1 Timothy 3:15 he writes, "If I am delayed, you will know how people ought to conduct themselves in God's household, which is the church of the living God, the pillar and foundation of the truth."

By referring to the church as "God's household," Paul expresses the family-like quality of the unity among believers. As God's children, we are part of the heavenly family. We are the bride of Christ, and God is our Father. We exist as brothers and sisters, and our first obligation is to each other.

For this reason, we are reminded in Hebrews 10:24 to "consider how we may spur one another on toward love and good deeds," and to "not give up meeting together, as some are in the habit of doing, but [to] encourage one another" (Hebrews 10:25).

The author of Hebrews makes the importance of accountability abundantly clear. The purpose of meeting together, he tells us, is to continually encourage one another. Furthermore, he urges us to not give up meeting together so we won't end up trapped in the deception of sin.

Clearly, meeting regularly with fellow Christians and holding each other accountable is vital to our spiritual growth. As Christians, we need both of these elements to grow, just as a plant needs sun and water.

Many church-goers are unwilling to acknowledge the importance of accountability among believers. As we discussed, they view it as a threat of privacy rather than a necessity of church life. In 1 Corinthians 5:12-14, Paul tells us of the importance of judging those inside the church: "Are you not to judge those inside?" he asks. "God will judge those outside. 'Expel the wicked man from among you.'" Similarly, the writer of Hebrews instructs us to "encourage one another daily" so we won't be "hardened by sin's deceitfulness" (Hebrews 3:13). Matthew 18:15-17 provides the order of events when confronting a sinful brother. Jesus tells us to show him his fault in private first, then to take one or two witnesses, and finally to tell the whole church if he isn't won over earlier in the process.

Without accountability in the church, the temptation to fall into sin's deceitfulness is strengthened immensely. The church must be unified to combat the enemy of sin, which Jesus made clear through His prayer to the Father to bring the church to "complete unity" in John 17:23, and which Paul reminds us in 1 Corinthians 12:13 when he states, "For we were all baptized by one Spirit into one body—whether Jews or Greeks, slave or free—and we were all given the one Spirit to drink." We are each a part of the church, which Paul points out in 1 Corinthians

12:27, and when one of us is missing, the church is weakened by our loss.

Jesus elaborates on the significance of each member of the church through a parable in Matthew 18:

> "What do you think? If a man owns a hundred sheep, and one of them wanders away, will he not leave the ninety-nine on the hills and go to look for the one that wandered off? And if he finds it, I tell you the truth, he is happier about that one sheep than about the ninety-nine that did not wander off. In the same way your Father in heaven is not willing that any of these little ones should be lost." (Matthew 18:12-24)

If you shirk your duty of going to church, the body is weakened by your absence. Jesus deems you so important that He would leave all the other obedient members to find you and bring you back to the flock. He desires you to be such an integral part of His church that He appoints you to lead it.

In Acts 20:28, Paul commands, "Keep watch over yourselves and all the flock of which the Holy Spirit has made you overseers. Be shepherds of the church of God, which he bought with his own blood."

In sharp contrast to a sheep gone astray, God wants you to be the shepherd who looks after the sheep of His church. By not attending, you are clearly a lost sheep. You have wandered away from the flock and have forced the true shepherds of the church to search for you and bring you back. But you are not supposed to be a wandering sheep; you are commanded to be a shepherd, leading the herd, encouraging those who would go astray to hold fast and be faithfully committed.

Unless you are a pastor, elder, or deacon, you may not feel like a legitimate leader of your church. You likely view yourself as just another face in the crowd with no obligation aside from the Sunday morning service or the occasional Wednesday evening prayer meeting. You may wonder how you are obligated or even qualified to be a shepherd rather than a sheep. But God charges you with a leadership role that is vital to maintaining unity in the church. He requires that you be an active presence in the life of the church so you may edify your brothers in Christ and spur them on in their faith.

A sad truth, that is every bit as devastating to the church as non-attendance, is the lack of participation among attending members. It is not enough to simply show up each Sunday morning. We are called to fulfill an active role as part of the church body, and each role is crucial to the strength of the church.

In 1 Corinthians 12:28, Paul says that "in the church God has appointed first of all apostles, second prophets, third teachers, then workers of miracles, also those having gifts of healing, those able to help others, those with gifts of administration, and those speaking in different kinds of tongues." Similarly, in Ephesians 4:11-12, he remarks, "It was [Jesus] who gave some to be apostles, some to be prophets, some to be evangelists, and some to be pastors and teachers, to prepare God's people for works of service, so that the body of Christ may be built up."

Each member of the church, according to Paul, possesses a unique God-given gift that is useful in the church. Not all will have the same gift, but each gift is valuable. "Are all apostles?" Paul rhetorically asks. "Are all prophets? Are all teachers? Do all work miracles? Do all have gifts of healing? Do all speak in tongues? Do all interpret" (1 Corinthians 12:29-30)?

As a Christian, you possess God-given talents that are useful in building up the church. Maybe you are a pastor. Perhaps you are an elder or deacon, or maybe a Sunday school teacher or Bible study leader. Maybe you are the church secretary, pianist, or one who makes weekly visits to nursing homes and hospitals to visit the sick.

Regardless of your particular role, your gifts are important and you are required to use them. You are not simply asked to use them—you are *commanded* to contribute your gifts for the betterment of the church. By being obedient to Christ's command to be active in the church, you are not only helping yourself and others, you are directly contributing to the Kingdom of Heaven and to Christ Himself. "'I tell you the truth, whatever you did for one of the least of these brothers of mine, you did for me'" Jesus declares (Matthew 25:40).

Can you think of a greater pleasure than to serve Christ? By building up the church—the very body of Christ—you are serving Him in obedience and storing up treasures for yourself in Heaven, as Jesus strongly encourages you to do in Matthew 6:20.

But how do you react when others in the church are not displaying the fruits of the spirit? What course of action is appropriate when church leadership is leading the congregation down a dangerous path?

Aside from the option of searching for a new church family if things become almost too broken to fix, you can take comfort in knowing that God holds those leaders accountable for their decisions. James 3:1 states, "Not many of you should presume to be teachers, my brothers, because you know that we who teach will be judged more strictly."

1 Timothy 3:1-7 and Titus 1:6-9 lay out the criteria for church leaders, and the qualifications one must possess to lead the church are all but easy to meet. God gives us these strict qualifications to ensure that the church remains strong. No

organization, including the church, can run efficiently without qualified officials who are in a position to properly govern it.

Similar to our governmental structure here in America, God has established a checks and balances system within the church so that wrongful authority can be challenged and stopped. 1 Timothy 5:19 urges us to "not entertain an accusation against an elder unless it is brought by two or three witnesses. Those who sin are to be rebuked publicly, so that the others may take warning."

Paul tells us to not be quick to charge an elder with an offense, because his position is an appointed and respectable one, but to rebuke him publicly if he is, indeed, at fault. Paul himself rebuked Peter "to his face" in front of the congregation at Antioch for hypocritically disassociating himself with the Gentiles, whom he had been fellowshipping with, in front of the Jews because they were part of the circumcision group. Paul asserts that Peter was "clearly in the wrong" (Galatians 2:11-17).

In the absence of clear wrongdoing, however, we are commanded to submit to our authorities:

> Everyone must submit himself to the governing authorities, for there is no authority except that which God has established. The authorities that exist have been established by God. (Romans 13:1)

> Submit yourselves for the Lord's sake to every authority instituted among men: whether to the king, as the supreme authority, or to governors, who are sent by him to punish those who do wrong and to commend those who do right. (1 Peter 2:13-14)

Obey your leaders and submit to their authority. They keep watch over you as men who must give an account. Obey them so that their work may be a joy, not a burden, for that would be of no advantage to you. (Hebrews 13:17)

How often do you find yourself making your pastor's life a burden rather than a joy? Hopefully never, but I have known so many pastors who have resigned their positions or moved to new churches because their congregations made their ministries dreadfully burdensome. Just as God appoints kings and other rulers into their positions, He appoints pastors into theirs, and it is the job of those under that authority to be supportive and encouraging of the shepherd God has appointed over His flock. Lack of such support fuels bitterness, which only causes trouble and ultimately defiles many (Heb. 12:15). If bitterness ensues, be sure to correct it with your brother immediately before it defiles the church. And instead of running from the situation, confront it head on with confidence in Christ, for no reason is grounds for disobeying God's command to build up His church.

You may feel hopeless in finding the right church, and you may have run into so much legalism and politics that you can't even imagine a church without them. But rather than run from those problems, it is your duty—your commission from Jesus himself—to help fix those problems by encouraging your brethren to focus on the cross and to flee from all sin. If your brother is lost, find him and bring him back to the flock where he belongs. Be a shepherd, not a sheep.

The church is an absolutely vital part of every believer's life. We need the church in a very literal way to grow spiritually through worship, the hearing of the word, edification, and fellowship with our Christian family. Sunday mornings are a weekly spiritual refresher that prepare us for the coming week, but our involvement should be so much more than just the ten o'clock Sunday morning service. I encourage you to not only attend church, but to become actively involved with your church family, for you are an important part of the church body and your gifts are extremely useful in building up the church. Do not be content with avoiding church because your salvation isn't based on attendance; be concerned with obeying Jesus' command to grow His church for the purpose of growing His kingdom. When you commit to this act of faithful obedience, you will learn that the church is, indeed, a necessity for any true, God fearing Christian.

Questions for Reflection

1. Have you ever stopped attending church for political or legalistic reasons? If so, would you do it again? Why or why not?

2. Have you hidden behind the excuse that you don't need to attend church to be a Christian? How legitimate do you view that excuse now?

3. Do you recognize the importance of being a part of a body of believers?

4. What are some of the primary reasons for participating in the church? Why are they necessary?

5. If you are not currently attending church, will you now? If you are currently attending but are not as involved as you should be, can you think of ways to utilize your gifts for the church?

9 | *"God Helps Those Who Help Themselves"*

Of all the quotations I will address in this book, "God helps those who help themselves" is probably the most overused of them all. This old aphorism is actually credited to Benjamin Franklin and first appeared in Poor Richard's Almanac in 1757. Today, two hundred and fifty years later, Christians quote this popular six-word phrase as if it were a proverb or a profound excerpt of Solomonic wisdom.

While this quotation warrants a degree of admiration for its attempt to encourage Christian self-initiative, it paints a very misleading portrait of God's role in our lives. When Ben Franklin first suggested that man's self-help needs to precede God's sovereign aid, He probably intended to communicate the need for Christian motivation and responsibility. Like many of us today, Mr. Franklin was probably disgusted by the lack of spiritual initiative he saw amidst humanity and sought to alleviate the problem with his words. I wonder, though, if he intended to downplay God's majesty and the significance of His grace.

My guess is that Ben Franklin did not intend to diminish God's authority, but that is exactly what many modern

Christians do when they improperly quote the phrase "God helps those who help themselves." The Bible makes it clear that God does not hold man blameless for his decisions, but in light of the fall, man is innately helpless and in need of God's assistance in all matters of life.

I have already addressed our helplessness when it comes to salvation. According to Romans 3, we are all sinners, dead in our trespasses, incapable of even desiring to choose Christ. Paul says in Romans 5:6 that "at just the right time, when we were still powerless, Christ died for the ungodly." In 2 Corinthians 5:21, he puts it another way: "God made him who had no sin to be sin for us, so that in him we might become the righteousness of God."

Without Christ's substitutionary death on the cross, we would be "powerless" to save ourselves, according to Paul. Jesus was forced "to be sin for us" because we were incapable of redeeming ourselves. God's effectual calling is absolutely necessary for anyone to come to a saving knowledge of Christ. But what about other areas of life? Are we completely helpless in even the smallest, most mundane tasks of daily living?

The degree of freedom God grants us is enough to render us capable of accomplishing ordinary tasks, but only under His providential sovereignty. As we discussed in Chapter 5, man is free to choose what he desires to an extent, but God retains ultimate control over everything in existence and nothing ever happens outside of His decreed, sovereign will. In other words, you are capable of doing many things at any given moment, but only because God allows you to do them. In John 15:5, Jesus explicitly states, "Apart from me you can do nothing."

Nothing can exist apart from God, for He is the creator of all things. His entire creation is subject to His control and heeds His every command. Even the sun, the moon, the stars, the wind, and all other creatures of the earth praise the name of the

Lord, Psalm 148 tells us. God breathes life into inanimate matter for the sheer purpose of praising Him and exalting His name.

All of creation hails its King, and we are no different. Just as the stars, the hills, the birds, and the trees depend entirely on their maker, we too depend on God for everything we have in life. We would have nothing apart from God's providence.

You may be wondering at this point what the words *providence* and *sovereignty* mean, so let's take a moment to become more familiar with each term.

God's *providence* is His divine care, direction, and management in our lives. When fortune befalls us, we know it is due to God's divine providence, not mere luck or chance. By "fortune," I do not mean wealth or fame, but blessings God bestows on us in light of the kind intention of His will. The word *sovereignty* refers to God's supreme authority and complete control. Kings are often labeled "sovereign" because their positions are exclusively authoritative, and God's sovereignty denotes His omnipotence and authoritative control over everything He has made. His sovereignty is not that of an earthly king, however; He is the King of Kings, the Lord of Lords, and His sovereignty reigns supreme.

It is important to note that God's providence and sovereignty do not only affect those who are saved. The reprobate experience occasional blessings the same way the elect do, and they are under God's sovereign hand the same way His children and the rest of the world are. Unsaved people cannot experience true joy and happiness apart from Christ, but they can experience moments of pleasure the same way believers can. Though they are not the children of God, their Creator still grants them moments of happiness as their earthly lives are the only semblance of happiness they will ever know.

Ultimately, everyone and everything is under God's control, and through His divine authority, God dictates the course of our lives—our beginning, our end, and everything in between. Because of this reality, we are totally helpless. Apart from God's providential assistance, we can do literally nothing.

"Then why not leave my life entirely in God's hands?" you might ask. "Why bother getting up in the morning if I have no real control over my own life?"

The answer to this question is that being helpless does not give you the right to be lazy. I have met many people who use God's sovereignty as a copout to avoid action and who hide behind it to excuse themselves from any responsibility.

The most common example is a Christian who has lost his job. He claims to trust that God will providentially provide another job and that he will simply wait for God to provide one in His own timing. In the meantime, he makes no attempt to find another position, and when nothing turns up he blames God for the failure and accepts no responsibility for his own lack of initiative.

While this man may be putting his trust in the Lord to aid in his career search, he is not doing his part to find another job. God will most assuredly provide another position for the unemployed worker (provided it is His will for the worker to work again), but not without the worker so much as searching for another career. In this case, the worker is using God's providence as an excuse to be lazy. He is attempting to force God's hand while neglecting his own God-given abilities to secure a new career for himself.

This is the exact type of case most Christians are addressing when they say that "God helps those who help themselves," and my assumption is that Benjamin Franklin quoted the phrase in the same vein. People quote Franklin's mantra to discourage this kind of lazy, irresponsible behavior that many professing Christians have found themselves falling into. In such instances, their attempts at gently rebuking their brethren are noble, but often times others remind that "God helps those who help themselves" for not so noble reasons.

Many so-called Christians spout off the old adage to suggest that we can "do it ourselves"—that we don't need God for everything—that we are perfectly capable of getting through most areas of life on our own.

Most often, those who think along these lines assume that they are not only being responsible by relying on their own abilities, but that they are pleasing God through their willingness and self-reliance as well. They feel that by taking on a heftier work load they remove some of God's burden (as if He can't handle it all on His own).

Little do they realize, God expects us to rely on Him and even desires us to. In demonstration of this fact, Jesus himself said, "I tell you the truth, the Son can do nothing by himself; he can do only what he sees his Father doing, because whatever the Father does the Son also does" (John 5:19). All throughout Scripture, we see Jesus submitting to the will of the Father, and in this particular case, Jesus' display of submission models that of humanity. Like Christ, we do nothing of our own accord. The Father must ordain all that we do.

In fact, any action not grounded in God is utterly useless, according to Scripture. Psalm 127 states, "Unless the LORD builds the house, its builders labor in vain. Unless the LORD watches over the city, the watchmen stand guard in vain."

Unfortunately, this verse is all too commonly overlooked. Here we read that God must be at the forefront of any endeavor in order for it to be successful. This verse mentions a house, a city, and watchmen, but it directly applies to every single element of life from the time it was penned to today. It acts as a synecdoche, a part put for the whole. It might as well read, "Unless the LORD is the head of something, that something will fail." God knows no defeat, only victory.

The almighty nature of God is one of the most comforting reassurances for Christians. Trusting in God's strength more than our own is a command, but it is also an incomprehensible pleasure that we can always find solace in. The Psalms, Isaiah, and Jeremiah constantly remind us of the comfort God provides to His children:

> You will increase my honor and comfort me once again. (Psalm 71:21)

> Give me a sign of your goodness, that my enemies may see it and be put to shame, for you, O LORD, have helped me and comforted me. (Psalm 86:17)

> May your unfailing love be my comfort. (Psalm 119:76)

> Although you were angry with me, your anger has turned away and you have comforted me. (Isaiah 12:1)

> For the LORD comforts his people and will have compassion on the afflicted ones. (Isaiah 49:13)

> For the LORD has comforted his people, he has redeemed Jerusalem. (Isaiah 52:9)

> As a mother comforts her child, so will I comfort you. (Isaiah 66:13)

> O my Comforter in sorrow, my heart is faint within me. (Jeremiah 8:18)

> I will give them comfort and joy instead of sorrow. (Jeremiah 31:13)

The list goes on, but these are just a few of the verses that identify God as our Comforter. How wonderful it is to see God as our refuge and hiding place, the one we can always trust in times of joy as well as distress.

God wants to be our comfort so that we will fully place our trust in Him and glorify Him for His continual provision. It is never our job to help ourselves. If anything, it is our duty as obedient followers of Christ to serve and help others. Our relationship with God is not indicative of one with a friend where you enter a friend's house and she tells you to "help yourself." God's promise as you enter His realm through prayer, Scripture, or fellowship is "I will help you."

His help is so dependable that Jesus instructs us to not worry about any aspect of our lives:

> Therefore I tell you, do not worry about your life, what you will eat or drink; or about your body, what you will wear. Is not life more important than food, and the body more important than clothes? Look at the birds of the air; they do not sow or reap or store away in barns, and yet your heavenly Father feeds them. Are you not much more valuable than they? Who of you by worrying can add a single

hour to his life? And…therefore do not worry about tomorrow, for tomorrow will worry about itself. Each day has enough trouble of its own. (Matthew 6:25-34)

The recurring theme in this passage and the others of this chapter is that God is in control. And in the words of the Apostle Paul, "If God is for us, who can be against us" (Romans 8:31)?

Paul's words shed a different light on God's nature than Benjamin Franklin's. Romans 8:31 marks God as our victorious warrior and protector, while Ben Franklin's famous aphorism sends the message that God idly sits around waiting for us to take action for ourselves before He will initiate any kind of help for us.

Christians have quoted the Franklin phrase with varying intentions, but regardless of their motives the phrase itself is fundamentally flawed. We are, indeed, responsible for our choices in life, but we are utterly helpless apart from the providence and sovereign aid of our Almighty God. The next time you run into a brother who insists that "God helps those who help themselves," confidently reply that "God helps those who *can't* help themselves" and kindly suggest that they read this chapter to gain clearer insight on the issue.

Questions for Reflection

1. What have you always thought the phrase "God helps those who help themselves" means?

2. Can you do anything apart from Christ, or are you completely helpless on your own? What does the Bible say?

3. Scripture presents God as both a fierce warrior and a gentle comforter. What do these attributes of God mean for you as a Christian?

10 | *"Don't Judge Me"*

Admit it. You've said it a million times. The most common response when someone rebukes us is "don't judge me."

This short, yet pointed defense works well in guarding our sins and excusing our poor actions. When we criticize others for "judging" us, we not only shield ourselves from correction, we remind those correcting us of their sins as well. In three words, we communicate the essence of a few notable passages. We act as Jesus instructing our accusers to cast the first stone if they are without sin. We remind them to remove the plank in their own eye before making us aware of the speck in ours. We indirectly label them hypocrites who dare to point out our sins while they are guilty of so many themselves.

Often times it is right to discourage judgment in light of the above-mentioned passages, but more often Jesus' command to not judge is misconstrued. The most popular passage on judgment is Matthew 7:1-2, in which Jesus commands, "Do not judge, or you too will be judged. For in the same way you judge others, and with the measure you use, it will be measured to you."

Many Christians interpret this passage to mean that we should never point out anyone else's sin because we are guilty of sin ourselves and are, therefore, not in a position to correct the iniquities of others. As wicked, depraved sinners, how can we claim the right to correct people no more wicked than ourselves?

In fact, we *do* have the right to correct others when they are in the wrong, but correcting them is not the same as judging them. This is a delicate subject, but it becomes much easier to decipher when you understand the difference between rebuking your brother and judging him.

Jesus commands us to refrain from judgment, but to the same degree He tells us to rebuke and correct our brothers in love. Judging, in the context in which Jesus uses the word, is wrongly accusing others of something without proof of their guilt. Calling a man who kills someone a murderer is not an act of judgment because the man is, by definition, a murderer. His title comes from fact, not assumption. On the other hand, accusing the murderer's son of murder, because his father is a killer, is an instance of judgment because the son did not commit the crime. To assume that the son is guilty of his father's sin without any evidence to support that assumption is to wrongfully judge him; and this type of action is what Jesus condemns.

What Jesus promotes and, in fact, demands is that we gently rebuke others when we find them in sin to encourage repentance and help spur them on in the faith. I already cited the most well-known passage on judgment from Matthew 7, so I'll provide a few more passages related to judgment that seem to convey a different message. Keep in mind that these passages do not contradict the seventh chapter of Matthew, but they differ in how sharply they address the need for correction. The first set of passages marks corrective judgment as a righteous tool:

> The mouth of the righteous man utters wisdom, and his tongue speaks what is just. (Psalm 37:30)

> Speak up and judge fairly; defend the rights of the poor and needy. (Proverbs 31:9)

> With my lips I recount all the laws that come from your mouth. (Psalm 119:13)

> Stop judging by mere appearances, and make a right judgment. (John 7:24)

Judgment is a righteous action, but only when it is properly administered. Righteous judgment fosters wisdom and justice, according to Psalm 37:30, a defense for the poor and needy, according to Proverbs 31:9, adherence to God's laws, according to Psalm 119:13, and the degradation of vanity, according to John 7:24. Judging others righteously is a habit the Lord expects us to adopt because making others aware of their sin brings them to penitence and enables them to grow spiritually. Here are a few passages where the Lord discusses this truth:

> Shout it aloud, do not hold back. Raise your voice like a trumpet. Declare to my people their rebellion and to the house of Jacob their sins. (Isaiah 58:1)

> Remember this: Whoever turns a sinner from the error of his way will save him from death and cover over a multitude of sins. (James 5:20)

> When I say to the wicked, "O wicked man, you
> will surely die," and you do not speak out to
> dissuade him from his ways, that wicked man will
> die for his sin, and I will hold you accountable for
> his blood.(Ezekiel 33:8)

The necessity to judge is so great that it must be shouted aloud so the sinner will be turned from his evil ways and saved from death. Furthermore, we will be held accountable for not rebuking others and encouraging them to repent of their wicked ways.

Confronting others about their sin, however, is an all but easy task. Rebuking too harshly often ignites anger and causes them to turn a deaf ear to your words rather than an open mind. On the other hand, rebuking them too gently may give them the false impression that their sins are not significant enough to warrant true repentance and a permanent change. The proper approach is delicate, but fortunately God gives us the best method to confront sinners in His Word:

> Preach the Word; be prepared in season and out of
> season; correct, rebuke and encourage—with great
> patience and careful instruction. (2 Timothy 4:2)

> Therefore, rebuke them sharply, so that they will
> be sound in the faith. (Titus 1:13)Encourage and
> rebuke with all authority. Do not let anyone despise
> you. (Titus 2:15)

> If your brother sins, rebuke him, and if he repents,
> forgive him. (Luke 17:3)

Each of these passages instructs us to rebuke others when they sin, but they provide us with some additional pointers as well. Our aim should be to encourage those we correct, 2 Timothy 4:2 and Titus 2:15 tell us. If our desire is to simply point out their sins with no intention of helping them, then we are committing an awful sin ourselves. Our stance should be bold and authoritative, but we should be patient and careful in how we instruct others so they will understand the error of their ways and commit themselves to living righteously. Our goal should be admonishment, which is gentle, yet earnest reproval. And most importantly, we must forgive others when they repent and ask forgiveness.

The ultimate goal of all correction is betterment. Just as a mother disciplines her children to lovingly encourage righteousness and maturity, God commands us to rebuke each other in love so that we will become increasingly righteous and spiritually mature. He causes us to judge all things so that we will avoid temptation and practice what is good. In 1 Corinthians, Paul describes the Christian practice of judging all things:

> The spiritual man makes judgments about all things, but he himself is not subject to any man's judgment. (1 Corinthians 2:15)

> Do you not know that the saints will judge the world? (1 Corinthians 6:2)

"Why, then," you might ask, "is it okay for Christians to judge all things?" And the answer to that question is, "Because God has already judged them."

The Lord has already passed judgment on all things and deemed them either good or evil, so when we pass judgment as Christians, it is in accordance with God's prior judgment, not our own blind assumption. We are able to judge because God has already established what is right and wrong and has written His law on our hearts and minds. As regenerated creatures, we possess knowledge of good and evil and are, therefore, qualified to judge all that we experience in life.

Ironically, the rest of the world does the exact same thing, in spite of its lack of godly wisdom. Human law is a set of rules that, in its most basic sense, establishes right from wrong and judges anyone who does not abide by the established order.

Judgment is of crucial importance, even to unsaved people, because of the likelihood of chaos without it. Without judgment, there would be no prisons for criminals because no one could be convicted, no order in schools or the workplace because no one's performance could be weighed against any sort of code, and no order in the home because parents could not measure the behavior of their children. Anyone could marry anyone or anything, false doctrine would spew forth from the pulpits in churches, and riots would line the streets with no resistance from law enforcement authorities. The process of judgment is so vital to daily living for the entire world that it should not be surprising how important it is to believers who are aliens in this world and obligated to witness in it.

Jesus demonstrated the importance of judging the world and rebuking its sin when He overturned the money tables at the temple. Matthew 21 vividly describes the scene:

> Jesus entered the temple area and drove out all who
> were buying and selling there. He overturned the
> tables of the money changers and the benches of

those selling doves. "It is written," he said to them, "My house will be called a house of prayer," but you are making it a "den of robbers." (Matthew 21:12-13)

The last thing anyone would have expected from Jesus was a public display like this. His rebuke was so intense that it bypassed the verbal stage and went straight to physical confrontation. No doubt Jesus' behavior was shocking to all who saw Him. His divine judgment rang loud and clear to all those who witnessed his dramatic reaction to the filthy, unholy corruption that poured through the temple walls. Jesus' judgment was righteous and acted as a powerful example of the effect of reproval. But Jesus is God and His judgments are always perfect. What about men? Do other biblical figures rebuke to this degree and provide an example the rest of us can follow?

If you recall from chapter 9, Paul publicly rebuked Peter in a similar fashion at Antioch. He sharply corrected Peter for hypocritically disassociating himself with the Gentiles in the presence of the Jews.

It is important to note that Peter was not just another member of the church. He was one of the original disciples and the first to ever confess faith in Christ as the Messiah. Jesus initiated His church with Peter and verbally granted him the keys to the kingdom of heaven in the presence of the other disciples. For this reason, Catholics consider Peter the first pope and have memorialized his name for centuries. Paul's public rebuke of Peter, then, was an event of colossal proportions, and it serves as a model for us today as we confront our brethren in the same way Paul did.

Paul claims his public rebuke of Peter was justified, but you may be wondering how Paul can make that claim in light of

Jesus' command to not pass judgment in the famous Matthew 7 passage. Paul even calls himself the worst of sinners in 1 Timothy 1:15, yet he dares to correct an apostle as notable as Peter.

Paul was, in fact, correct in rebuking Peter, and here is why: Paul was not committing the same sin he rebuked Peter for, so his judgment was not hypocritical. This foundational truth is where a proper understanding of biblical judgment begins. At the beginning of the chapter, we took a look at Matthew 7, where Jesus warns against passing judgment. We then proceeded to dissect a number of passages that seemed to contradict Jesus' words by encouraging us to judge all things and rebuke others when they sin. So how do we justify the apparent contradiction? What did Jesus mean when He warned us not to judge others? And what are we to think when we read the complete opposite in so many other places?

Read carefully. In Matthew 7, Jesus is not telling us to never rebuke those we find at fault. If He were, He would be contradicting another statement He made in which He warned, "Do not give dogs what is sacred; do not throw your pearls to pigs" (Matthew 7:6). Jesus' warning, rather, is to not judge hypocritically—to not chastise someone for committing a sin that you yourself are guilty of. Paul echoes Jesus' command in Romans 2:3 when he says, "So when you, a mere man, pass judgment on them and yet do the same things, do you think you will escape God's judgment?"

Put simply, hypocritical judgment is diabolical and righteous judgment is godly. Matthew 7 and Romans 2:3 do not warn against all judgment, just hypocritical judgment that is rooted in sin. Righteous judgment is a daily routine in the life of a believer, and as Christians, God grants us the ability to spiritually appraise all things and to lovingly correct sinners for their spiritual good.

The ability to judge is a powerful and necessary tool, and one that is so often misconstrued in the modern church. It has become a defense for sinners more than a weapon for the righteous, and countless verses have been neglected in favor of a couple that seem to label judgment as an act of evil. Judgment is evil when it is passed hypocritically, but when judgment is passed in righteousness and for the purpose of loving encouragement, it is not only a holy act, it is an act of obedience to Christ.

Be bold as Paul was with Peter. Be dramatic as Jesus was in the temple. But be careful to never be hypocritical as you pass judgment on others.

Questions for Reflection

1. Have you ever scolded others for judging you? If so, was their judgment of you righteous or hypocritical?

2. What type of judgment were Jesus and Paul referring to in Matthew 7:1-2 and Romans 2:3, respectively?

3. Which form of judgment are we commanded to continually engage in? How often, and to what extent?

4. Rebuking others in righteousness is a difficult assignment to be sure, but how do you plan on being obedient to Christ in this manner? Why is it so crucial for you to judge all things and to rebuke your Christian brethren?

11 | *"Unconditional Love"*

With so much talk about righteous judgment, it is hard to begin a chapter on the topic of the nature of God's love. God's characteristics of judgment and wrath seem to so sharply contrast His loving nature that transitioning from one set of attributes to the other seems almost counterintuitive.

For this reason, most Christians conveniently avoid the former issues and focus their attention entirely on God's love. They bask in their romantic ideals of God's love and exaggerate it to near unimaginable degrees. Their exaggeration is not faulty, mind you, when they are discussing God's love in relation to His elect. For God's chosen people, His love is truly unconditional. But the attainment of that love is initially based in conditions, and even if God has any shred of love for the unsaved, it is most certainly not unconditional.

God's love has been labeled unconditional in order to exaggerate its extent. The word *unconditional* simply means "without condition," so to call God's love unconditional is to say that God loves His children regardless of what they do.

It is Scripturally evident that no work can save us. We are saved through grace by faith alone in Christ, apart from any human effort. In Ephesians 2:8-9, Paul declares, "For it is by grace you have been saved, through faith—and this not from yourselves, it is the gift of God—not by works, so that no one can boast." He similarly reminded the Galatians of this fact:

You foolish Galatians! Who has bewitched you? Before your very eyes Jesus Christ was clearly portrayed as crucified. I would like to learn just one thing from you: Did you receive the Spirit by observing the law, or by believing what you heard? Are you so foolish? After beginning with the Spirit, are you now trying to attain your goal by human effort? Have you suffered so much for nothing—if it really was for nothing? Does God give you his Spirit and work miracles among you because you observe the law, or because you believe what you heard? (Galatians 3:1-5)

Clearly, our works are not what save us. We are saved through faith in Christ alone and Paul goes so far as to call any other assumption foolish. The very reason we praise God for our salvation is that He chose to love us and send His only son to die for us when we didn't deserve it and were utterly incapable of redeeming ourselves. Our salvation is completely unmerited, which proves the depths of God's love for those who put their faith in Him.

Our Father's love is incomprehensibly perfect for those who are saved. At the moment of salvation, God adopts us into His kingdom for all eternity. He blots out our transgressions, replaces our hearts of stone with hearts of flesh (Ezekiel 36:26), and erases our sin from His mind:

"I, even I, am he who blots out your transgressions, for my own sake, and remembers your sins no more." (Isaiah 43:25)

"For I will forgive their wickedness and will remember their sins no more." (Hebrews 8:12)

Once we are truly saved, there is nothing that can separate us from God's love. In the famous eighth chapter of Romans, Paul proclaims, "For I am convinced that neither death nor life, neither angels nor demons, neither the present nor the future, nor any powers, neither height nor depth, nor anything else in all creation, will be able to separate us from the love of God that is in Christ Jesus our Lord" (Romans 8:38-40). In other words, just as no good work can save us, no evil work can unsave us or cause God to stop loving us once we are saved. In this sense, God's love may be considered unconditional, in that no condition—no error we commit—will cause Him to revoke His love for us. As new creatures, born again, we are not even capable of sinning to the extent that God would desire to remove His love from us. His love is not based on any set of conditions, but purely in our faith for no other reason than the kind intention of His will.

The term *unconditional love* does not appear in the Bible, but as I pointed out earlier with the trinity, a term is not necessarily discredited simply because it does not appear in the text. If it can be reasonably inferred and proven, it should be given consideration as a valid assumption. In this case, the term *unconditional love* most likely arose out of confusion with John Calvin's term *unconditional election,* but the notion of unconditional love is appropriate when referring to the nature of God's love for the elect. It is not, however, appropriate when referring to His love for the rest of the world or when one attempts to make the argument that no conditions exist for those who would believe.

God's love for the whole world is debatable to begin with, so to call any love the Lord may have for those who are not saved "unconditional" is downright ridiculous. The difficult question is whether God's love for those who are saved is unconditional even before they are saved. We know from Scripture that God has predestined those who choose Him before the foundations of the world (Romans 8:29-30, Ephesians 1:5, 11). We also know that His love for us is, indeed, unconditional in its nature once we are saved. But does God love us unconditionally before we accept Christ?

Salvation itself is based in condition. It is a covenant whereby God guarantees that He will save us for all eternity based on the condition that we repent of our sins, accept Christ, and devote our lives to faithfully serving Him. God's promises always follow this pattern. All throughout Scripture, the Lord says, "If you do this in obedience to me, I will do this in response to your obedience." Salvation is just one of these instances, and it happens to be the most important.

The key condition that must be met in the salvation scenario is repentance, but unfortunately many professing Christians do not wish to acknowledge repentance as a requisite for God's love. Because they view God's love as unconditional at all stages of a believer's life, they feel as though no conditions must be met at any point during the redemptive process. Often times such people even regard God's love as unconditional for unbelievers.

This is a sad error on the part of those who believe such heresies because such a mindset will inevitably lead to damnation. To view God's love as completely unconditional for all people at all times erases the need for salvation altogether. If God loved everyone unconditionally at all times, there would have been no need for Christ and everyone would go to Heaven without even attempting to lead godly lives.

The good news is, for those who do seek God and meet His conditions for salvation, His love *is* unconditional. We delight in the Lord's love for us as He recounts, "I have loved you with an everlasting love; I have drawn you with loving-kindness" (Jeremiah 31:3). We find comfort in John's words as he tells us that "God is love" (1 John 4:8).

For those who have put their trust in Christ as their Savior and accepted God's free gift of grace, the depths of God's love are boundless. His love for His children is intentional, unmerited, and ultimately unconditional. For those who reject Christ, the opposite is true.

Unrepentant sinners often define God's unconditional love as a love He grants sinners irrespective of their love for Him. They see God's love as unconditional in the sense that He loves everyone in spite of their lack of faith in Him. This diabolical heresy goes way beyond the notion that God loves everyone equally. The Bible explicitly teaches that salvation requires love for the Lord. Let's take a look at how the Bible portrays the need to love the Lord in order to be saved:

Love the LORD your God with all your heart and with all your soul and with all your strength. (Deuteronomy 6:5)

Know therefore that the LORD your God is God; he is the faithful God, keeping his covenant of love to a thousand generations of those who love him and keep his commands. (Deuteronomy 7:9)

So be very careful to love the LORD your God. (Joshua 23:11)

Then I said: "O LORD, God of heaven, the great and awesome God, who keeps his covenant of love

with those who love him and obey his commands."
(Nehemiah 1:5)

Love the LORD, all his saints! The LORD
preserves the faithful, but the proud he pays back
in full. (Psalm 31:23)

The LORD loves righteousness and justice; the
earth is full of his unfailing love. (Psalm 33:5)

For the LORD loves the just and will not forsake
his faithful ones. They will be protected forever,
but the offspring of the wicked will be cut off.
(Psalm 37:28)

For as high as the heavens are above the earth, so
great is his love for those who fear him. (Psalm
103:11)

The LORD watches over all who love him, but all
the wicked he will destroy. (Psalm 145:20)

The LORD detests the way of the wicked but he
loves those who pursue righteousness. (Proverbs
15:9)

Contrary to what many people believe, these verses make it
abundantly clear that God's love is not directed toward
everyone and that those whom the Lord loves must love Him in
return.

The above verses establish specific characteristics of those
who love God. Such people love God with all their heart, soul,

and strength. They love and keep His commands. They are faithful, righteous, and just. And they fear Him and pursue what is good.

The wicked, however, endure the torments of God's wrath. The Lord detests their ways. He will pay them back in full, their offspring will be cut off, and they will be destroyed.

God's benevolent love is reserved only for those who love Him and obey His commands. If you do not love the Lord, you will endure His righteous judgment in place of His unfailing love. Your salvation is unmerited and is the result of God's initial love for you, but it is granted to you on the basis of the condition that you accept God's free gift of grace in Christ. At the moment you repent and turn to Christ, you enter into an eternal covenant with the Lord and discover what God's unconditional love truly is.

Questions for Reflection

1. How's is God's love unconditional? How is it not?

2. Who experiences God's unconditional love?

3. Although the term *unconditional love* does not appear in the Bible, is it reasonably inferred from the text? In what case?

12 | "Being a Christian Means Being Tolerant"

A few weeks ago I attended a church service out of town and the sermon happened to be on the issue of tolerance. The pastor paced at his pulpit, grinning ear to ear as he confidently stressed to the congregation the importance of being tolerant as Christians. This was the Sunday after the Virginia Tech massacre and his sermon was very intentional in communicating the message of tolerance. "This gunman obviously had a few screws loose," he jokingly remarked, "but as Christians we should all remember the importance of tolerating all people regardless of their actions."

Needless to say, I left that Sunday service shocked by what I had heard. The last thing I expected to hear was a pastor saying it is right for Christians to be tolerant of sin. Romans 6:23 immediately came to mind where Paul writes, "For the wages of sin is death, but the gift of God is eternal life in Christ Jesus our Lord" (Romans 6:23).

I have already addressed the incredible importance of righteously judging and rebuking our brothers and sisters who fall into sin. The wages of an impenitent heart is not temporary punishment or a quick slap on the wrist—it is death! By not making clear the wages of sin and the certainty of spending an eternity in Hell without forsaking them, we are not preaching the Gospel or showing others the love of Christ.

But where does tolerance come into play? Aren't we, as Christians, supposed to exercise tolerance? Isn't tolerating others an act of Christian love? After all, Jesus ate with the most wretched of sinners and Paul talks of becoming all things to all men in 1 Corinthians 9:21-23.

But why did Jesus and Paul do such things? In the same passage in 1 Corinthians, Paul states his reason for becoming all things to all men. He says, "To those not having the law I became like one not having the law (though I am not free from God's law but am under Christ's law), so as to win those not having the law. To the weak I became weak, to win the weak. I have become all things to all men *so that by all possible means I might save some.* I do all this *for the sake of the gospel,* that I may share in its blessings."

Neither Jesus nor Paul ever tolerated the sin of the heathens they socialized with. Rather, they made them aware of the wages of their ungodliness and led them to repentance so they might be saved. When Paul says he became like sinners, he does not mean he adopted their sinful practices; if that's what he meant he could not call himself a Christian. Rather, he means he befriended sinners, came into their circle, and grew close enough to them to share the Gospel and lead them to Christ.

Many of today's churches do not follow Paul's and Christ's example. So many denominations of the modern church have tragically misinterpreted what it means to witness and to exhibit the love of Christ. They think becoming like sinners means accepting their sin rather than merely becoming close to them as a means of leading them to Christ.

A friend of mine was recently asked to sing for the baptism of a gay couple's adopted baby at a local Methodist church. In this case, the church didn't only tolerate the sin of the couple— they actually condoned and encouraged it! When the church should have been sharply rebuking the couple for their wicked relationship and their attempt to bring a child into it, they were instead providing the very venue for them to carry out their evil scheme.

Nowhere in Scripture do we read that we are to tolerate sin. On the contrary, we read countless times that we are to battle unrighteousness wherever it rears its ugly head. We are commanded to be kind and gentle toward others in an effort to show them Christ's love and to bring them to penitence so they may avoid damnation and come to a saving knowledge of Christ. But gentility and kindness are very different from tolerance.

To tolerate something is to put up with it. There is an element of recognition of wrongfulness imbedded within tolerance. That is, to say you "tolerate" something means you recognize it is wrong but allow it to continue anyway. Tolerance is essentially the allowance of sin.

In chapters three and ten I referenced a plethora of verses that expose the evil of tolerating others' sins. The danger in allowing others to continue living a life of rebellion against God is that they will never understand the error of their ways or their need for atonement through Christ. If they do not recognize the wages of their sin, they will not understand the need for repentance or redemption and will, thus, never be saved.

In this sense, tolerance is more an act of hatred than love. In tolerating your brother, you might as well be damning him to Hell. Remember the words from Ezekiel 33:8: "When I say to the wicked, 'O wicked man, you will surely die,' and you do not speak out to dissuade him from his ways, that wicked man will die for his sin, and I will hold you accountable for his blood." What a powerful verse! You must go even to the extent of warning the wicked of death if they do not repent. If you tolerate your brother's sin, you are responsible for his death in a very real way.

It is important to note that when I discuss tolerance in a biblical context I am referring to the tolerance of sin and nothing else. Today, the word *tolerance* has become popularized in all spheres—political, social, sexual, artistic, and the like. With so many areas, it can be challenging to decipher where tolerance should play a role and where it should not exist at all.

The easiest method for determining where tolerance should be exercised is to simply evaluate where sin is a factor. Clearly, it is right to tolerate ethnicity, gender, and other physical attributes of which people have no control. There is nothing sinful about being African American, Caucasian, Indian, or Chinese, just as there is nothing sinful about being a female instead of a male. On the other hand, sin inevitably invades politics, sexuality, and other intangible spheres and it is right to not exercise tolerance in these areas. The sins of a corrupt government should not be tolerated by its citizens, nor should the immoral marriage of a homosexual couple like the one mentioned earlier. God establishes the standards for right and wrong in His Word, and any disobedience of those standards is completely unacceptable in His eyes and should not be tolerated by God's children.

The standards God provides completely abolish all tolerance of sin. I have met many people who contend that everyone should be entitled to their own set of beliefs and should wholly accept and respect the beliefs of others. They define tolerance as respectful acceptance of varying sets of ideals.

This philosophy, however, is absurdity to true Christians. Respectfully accepting heresy and false doctrine is not part of our job description. Almighty God commissions us to preach truth to all corners of the earth and to *never* accept deceptions that will lead souls to Hell. I have been in many intense confrontations with non-Christians because they despise my unwillingness to back down from a religious argument. They demand that I respect and tolerate their beliefs and that I not attempt to force my own beliefs upon them. One person even said to me during a friendly discussion, "I like you and consider you my friend, but if you say one more word I will never speak to you again."

Unfortunately for people like this man, I heed the commandments of God before those of men. At times, I may need to adjust my approach to win someone over, but I will never give up or willingly allow someone caught in a web of deception to remain ensnared in it. My love for my fellow man is too great to see him burn in Hell for eternity, and I stand firm in the truth God has armed me with in converting the lost.

A major deterrence to the Gospel is man's expectation to never endure suffering and to always live in joy. Tolerance is one of many mechanisms that attempt to fuel this deterrence. The reality is that as Christians the Bible informs us that we will always face persecution for the Lord's sake and will inevitably endure trials and suffering as we grow in our spiritual maturity through sanctification. The following three verses echo this reality:

> For it has been granted to you on behalf of Christ not only to believe on him, but also to suffer for him. (Philippians 1:29)

> In fact, everyone who wants to live a godly life in Christ Jesus will be persecuted. (2 Timothy 3:12)

> Consider it pure joy, my brothers, whenever you face trials of many kinds, because you know that the testing of your faith develops perseverance. Perseverance must finish its work so that you may be mature and complete, not lacking anything. (James 1:2-4)

> Blessed are those who are persecuted because of righteousness, for theirs is the kingdom of heaven. "Blessed are you when people insult you, persecute you and falsely say all kinds of evil against you because of me. Rejoice and be glad, because great is your reward in heaven, for in the same way they persecuted the prophets who were before you." (Matthew 5:10-11)

As Christians, we should expect to be persecuted, but rather than lose heart, we should rejoice when others persecute us, knowing our heavenly reward is great and that our suffering produces spiritual maturity. Jesus tells us to "rejoice and be glad," and in James we are encouraged to "consider it pure joy" when we "face trials of many kinds."

Our spiritual growth is similar to our physical growth. When we lift weights, our muscles tear and then rebuild stronger than they were before. In the same way, when we experience trials and endure a spiritual workout, our faith rebuilds and grows stronger than it was.

One of the easiest ways to exercise your faith and to see persecution manifested is to rebuke others when they sin.

Intolerance is a recipe for persecution in a Christians' life. The more you battle sin, the more it battles back. The bolder you are in lovingly correcting others, the fiercer they will be in defending themselves. The more you live for the Gospel, the more you will face persecution. The challenge of living for the Gospel is all but easy, but it is the solemn vow of every born again believer (and for good reason.)

Let's go back for a moment to Paul's reason for becoming like all men from I Corinthians 9. Paul cites two reasons in this passage for becoming like sinners. The first is to "by all possible means...save some." The second reason is "for the sake of the gospel" and "to share in its blessings." Paul points out here that by spreading the Gospel of Christ he becomes a fellow partaker of it. He is a team player, so to speak, and is conveniently always on the winning side. Winning may not be easy, but Paul remains focused on the prize at the end of the race.

Where does your focus lie? Do you have your eyes fixed on the prize to come or on the hardships of today? Are you a team player like Paul, or do you run a solo act?

If you are habitually tolerant of sin, you are not a team player. By allowing your fellow man to continue on in his sin, you are helping him to die rather than live. The truth is that tolerance is only useful when the thing you are tolerating is not sinful. You should be careful to always be gentle and loving toward others in an effort to promote unity in the body of Christ. As Paul writes, "Brothers, if someone is caught in a sin, you who are spiritual should restore him gently. But watch yourself, or you also may be tempted. Carry each other's burdens, and in this way you will fulfill the law of Christ" (Galatians 6:1-2).

"Carry each other's burdens," Paul says. Help each other, endure trials with each other, grow with one another... But do not be tolerant of each other's sins.

Questions for Reflection

1. What does being tolerant really mean?

2. What types of tolerance should be practiced by Christians? What types should be avoided?

3. What does it mean to be a team player like Paul? How can we "become like all men?"

4. We should never be tolerant of sin, but how should we approach a brother who is caught in sin?

13 | *"God Understands"*

Have you ever shirked your Christian duties and claimed that God understands? If so, you would be one of millions. This two-word idiom is a favorite among professing Christians who really serve the world rather than God.

The copout "God understands" may be applied to any obligation we neglect to render us blameless for not fulfilling our obligations as servants of God. Any time I neglect to read the Word, pray, tithe, witness, or do anything else God has commanded of me, the easiest excuse to spout off is that God understands my inability to do what He requires of me.

Part of the reason it is so convenient to use "God understands" as an excuse is that the phrase makes God seem lenient. We hear two comforting words and suddenly our spiritual negligence seems perfectly acceptable to us (and we think to God as well.)

On the contrary, God never once tells us that He understands spiritual laziness or disobedience. He gives us commands and He expects us to obey them. Period.

But serving a life of total servitude to God can be very challenging, especially now when life seems so fast-paced and strenuous. Our earthly lives require so much of us that it seems we hardly even have time to devote as much to God as He expects. This is precisely why so many Christians say that God understands their lack of devotion. They reason that since He created the world and has control over it, He must surely recognize that the world consumes our lives and leaves us with very little time to devote to Him.

Knowing how difficult our earthly lives would be, God generously decided to actually require very little of us. He instructs us to be in His Word daily, to pray without ceasing, to be committed to one another, to strive to be like Christ, to tithe ten percent of our income, to spread the Gospel, and to generally be Christ-like in all that we do. It sounds like a lot. God does, in fact, give us many commands, but most of them come naturally from the Holy Spirit indwelling within us.

As born again creatures, we are totally regenerated and possess every ability to carry out God's revealed will. But while we are made anew and are no longer slaves to sin, sin is still a very real presence in our lives and one that poses a continual threat to our faithfulness. Sin's lordship over us is replaced by God's, but the power of sin still tries to control us. Sin still wants to be our master.

The Bible personifies sin by calling it the "flesh" and makes it clear that as Christians we are in the midst of a constant spirit-flesh battle (Galatians 5:17). Just as Newton noted that in physics every action has an equal and opposite reaction, our attempt to work for the Spirit has an equal and opposite reaction from the flesh, and vice versa. Any time you strive to do good, sin is right there discouraging you with equal force. Contrarily, whenever you engage in a sinful act, the Spirit will set in and cause your convictions to deter you from evil. Read Kris Lundgaard's book *The Enemy Within* to gain a clear understanding of the spirit-flesh struggle and the best methods for defeating sin.

The spirit-flesh battle is depicted extremely well in the old angel and devil on the shoulders scene. We've all seen these comical moments in cartoons and movies—the angel is always the person's conscious while the devil is always the carnal desire, or the "Id," in Freudian terms. The angel represents the spirit, and the devil represents the flesh.

The popular scene may be comical, but it really is an accurate portrayal of the inner workings of every believer. The spirit-flesh battle is one that rages inside every follower of Christ, and though we possess the ability to win the battles, we sometimes lose them.

I spoke with a pastor once who insisted that it is possible to never sin as a Christian. He reasoned that since Jesus told sinners to "go and sin no more," it must be possible to never sin because Jesus wouldn't have said it otherwise. This statement is so far removed from biblical truth that I won't even address it here, but the reality is that Jesus never suggests that we do things—He commands that we do them. He never says "go and try to sin no more;" He commands, "Go and sin no more." Jesus knows very well that it is impossible for anyone to never sin, but He does not give us free reign to do it. The flesh will win from time to time, and sometimes often, but God does not "understand" when we sin.

The good news is that He has already forgiven us of all our sins—past, present, and future, so while He doesn't "understand" and approve of our sin, He forgives it and does not hold it against us. We do, however, hold God's commands against Him when we excuse our spiritual laziness by claiming He understands.

There are so many instances in which it is easier to say that

God understands our inability to do what He wants than to simply do it. Your job may be very demanding, and the last thing you want to do after a hard day's work is open your Bible or pray. You may be struggling financially, so you decide to stop tithing for a few months until you get your finances back in order. You may be up late with a newborn baby every Saturday night and feel too tired in the morning to get up and go to church. In all of these cases, you excuse yourself by saying that God surely understands your situation and sympathizes with your plight.

The tragic flaw in this line of thinking is that it revolves around doubt and faithlessness instead of trust and faithfulness. If you trust in God and have faith that He will provide for you, you will be faithful in returning to God what is His through tithing. If you have faith in God to keep you healthy, you will go to church in spite of your fatigue. God rewards faithfulness, not laziness.

The parable of the talents demonstrates this fact:

> "Again, it will be like a man going on a journey, who called his servants and entrusted his property to them. To one he gave five talents of money, to another two talents, and to another one talent, each according to his ability. Then he went on his journey. The man who had received the five talents went at once and put his money to work and gained five more. So also, the one with the two talents gained two more. But the man who had received the one talent went off, dug a hole in the ground and hid his master's money. After a long time the master of those servants returned and settled accounts with them. The man who had received

the five talents brought the other five. 'Master,' he said, 'you entrusted me with five talents. See, I have gained five more.' His master replied, 'Well done, good and faithful servant! You have been faithful with a few things; I will put you in charge of many things. Come and share your master's happiness!' The man with the two talents also came. 'Master,' he said, 'you entrusted me with two talents; see, I have gained two more.' His master replied, 'Well done, good and faithful servant! You have been faithful with a few things; I will put you in charge of many things. Come and share your master's happiness!' Then the man who had received the one talent came. 'Master,' he said, 'I knew that you are a hard man, harvesting where you have not sown and gathering where you have not scattered seed. So I was afraid and went out and hid your talent in the ground. See, here is what belongs to you.' His master replied, 'You wicked, lazy servant! So you knew that I harvest where I have not sown and gather where I have not scattered seed? Well then, you should have put my money on deposit with the bankers, so that when I returned I would have received it back with interest. Take the talent from him and give it to the one who has the ten talents. For everyone who has will be given more, and he will have an abundance. Whoever does not have, even what he has will be taken from him. And throw that worthless servant outside, into the darkness, where there will be weeping and gnashing of teeth.'" (Matthew 25:14-30)

The last servant's wickedness was rooted in his unwillingness to serve his master out of fear and lack of faith. When we hide behind the excuse that God understands, we are no different from the wicked servant. We do what we feel comfortable doing because we fear that God's ways are not really best for us. Like the lazy servant, we trust ourselves more than our Master and do just enough to get by. We devote only as much time to God as we feel we must in order to stay in His good graces.

About a year ago, my wife and I were house hunting and one of the houses we toured belonged to an Islamic couple. We noticed that off the bedroom there was a small room, but it was not the bathroom and it was too big to be a typical walk-in closet. As we stepped into the room, we saw a decorative pillow on the floor beside what appeared to be a small wooden altar. Above the set-up was a sign on the wall that said "Remember to pray everyday."

After leaving the house, I couldn't stop thinking about that couple's dedication to their faith. As Christians, we have a room in our house for every normal task of daily living. We have a kitchen to cook in, a bathroom to bathe and waste in, a kitchen to cook in, a dining room to eat in, a bedroom to sleep in, an office to study in, a basement or attic to store things in, and a family room to gather and entertain ourselves in. We have a room for every single part of our lives, yet I don't know one Christian who has a room that is completely dedicated to the *most* important part—our relationship with God.

Even our houses demonstrate our faith in the world above Christ. Of course, we can pray, read, or fellowship in any room of a house, but the fact remains that we focus very little of our attention on our spiritual lives when compared to our earthly lives.

God should be our top priority, not the last thing on our list. Viewing Him as the least of our concerns is a devastating mistake, as it warps our proper perspective of God. It is easy to excuse ourselves from all kinds of sin and to fall into worldliness when we view God as one who doesn't really care what we do and who understands when we devote the least amount of our time to Him. Viewing Him for what He should really be—our number one priority and the one we dedicate most of our time to—is not quite as convenient. It requires faith that God's will for your life is better than your own and trust that His methods for your growth are better than any you could devise. God does understand that He should be our top priority and nothing less, and we should understand how important that reality truly is.

Questions for Reflection

1. Think of all the times you have shirked your Christian duties and used the excuse that "God understands."

2. What is wrong with hiding behind the "God understands" copout? Does it produce faithfulness or laziness?

3. Where should God sit on your list of priorities? Toward the bottom or at the very top?

4. What can you do to ensure that God retains the number one spot on your list?

14 | *"Your Best Life Now"*

When Joel Osteen published his best-selling book *Your Best Life Now: 7 Steps to Living at Your Full Potential* in October of 2004, the book took the Christian world by storm. Osteen's extraordinarily popular book, along with his other works and sermons, promote an appealing message of overcoming obstacles and achieving victory in life. Joel Osteen's congregation at Lakewood Church in Texas is the largest congregation in the United States, boasting a staggering thirty thousand members who pour into a renovated stadium each Sunday morning to hear the motivating words of a lost blind guide.

Not all of what Osteen writes in his book is heresy, but the basic premise of his message is diabolical in that it focuses on worldly victory rather than victory in Christ.

Your Best Life Now is essentially a blueprint for achieving success on earth—a theology referred to now as the prosperity gospel. Each page of the book is lined with fast-track methods for obtaining wealth, fame, happiness, and other forms of worldly success, and Mr. Osteen justifies each of these desires by saying that God wants all of these things for us. On page 5 he writes, "God wants to increase you financially, by giving you promotions, fresh ideas, and creativity." On the same page he claims, "God wants this to be the best time of your life." On page 35 he states, "God wants to give you your own house. God has a big dream for your life." Finally, he sums up his message on page 38 by saying, "God wants to make your life easier. He wants to assist you, to promote you, to give you advantages. He wants you to have preferential treatment."

Wow! What an inspiring (and completely deceitful) set of beliefs. With motivation like this, it's no surprise that Joel Osteen's congregation is the largest in America. What could possibly be better than being spoon fed a feel good sermon week after week as you are brainwashed into believing that God's plan for your life is imbedded in total joy and worldly success?

Earlier in the book I referenced Pastor Fred Phelps, the senior pastor of the notorious Westboro Baptist Church in Topeka, Kansas. The WBC is hated by nearly everyone in America because its congregation is extremely bold in publicly addressing sin. They have picketed thousands of churches, conferences, and even funerals of people who have either lived a life of sin or a life in support of it, and the signs they use are both shocking and offensive to the people they are directed to.

One sign you may see at their pickets says "Your pastor is a whore," and a video on their website justifies the sign by contending that the modern church is directly comparable to a prostitute because it does what a prostitute does: it provides a service that feels good for a fee. As long as money is pouring into the offering plates, the pastor will continue preach sermons that make the congregation feel good and convince them that it's okay to continue living in sin. Eager ears yearn to hear about ways to live for now, rather than eternity, to live for this world instead of the next (2 Timothy 4:3-4). But for a believer, living for now is the exact opposite of what the Bible instructs us to do.

Your best life as a believer is not "now" at all—it is the life to come in eternal paradise and glory with the Lord. Ephesians 2:7 encourages us to fix our eyes on the blessings to come, not the temporal rewards of today, for as David reminds us in Psalm 39, 89, and 144, and as we read in James 4:14, our days are fleeting and our earthly lives are like "a mist that appears for a little while and then vanishes." Our allegiance should belong solely to Christ, and as aliens in this world (1 Peter 2:11), we should despise the world in all its sin. The Bible continually emphasizes the innately sinful nature of the world and how we are to not desire worldly things:

> Those who live according to the sinful nature have their minds set on what that nature desires; but those who live in accordance with the Spirit have their minds set on what the Spirit desires. The mind of sinful man is death, but the mind controlled by the Spirit is life and peace; the sinful mind is hostile to God. It does not submit to God's law, nor can it do so. Those controlled by the sinful nature cannot please God. (Romans 8:5-8)

> But the Scripture declares that the whole world is a prisoner of sin, so that what was promised, being given through faith in Jesus Christ, might be given to those who believe. (Galatians 3:22)

> Godly sorrow brings repentance that leads to salvation and leaves no regret, but worldly sorrow brings death. (2 Corinthians 7:10)

We have not received the spirit of the world but the Spirit who is from God, that we may understand what God has freely given us. (1 Corinthians 2:12)

For the wisdom of this world is foolishness in God's sight. (1 Corinthians 3:19)

When we are judged by the Lord, we are being disciplined so that we will not be condemned with the world. (1 Corinthians 11:32)

For the grace of God that brings salvation has appeared to all men. It teaches us to say "No" to ungodliness and worldly passions, and to live self-controlled, upright and godly lives in this present age. (Titus 2:11-12)

"Woe to the world because of the things that cause people to sin! Such things must come, but woe to the man through whom they come!" (Matthew 18:7)

"If the world hates you, keep in mind that it hated me first. If you belonged to the world, it would love you as its own. As it is, you do not belong to the world, but I have chosen you out of the world. That is why the world hates you." (John 15:18-19)

For our struggle is not against flesh and blood, but against the rulers, against the authorities, against the powers of this dark world and against the spiritual forces of evil in the heavenly realms. (Ephesians 6:12)

The world is a literal melting pot of sin, and it is foreign territory to the children of God. Christians are playing an away game during their lives on earth, patiently awaiting their return home. In playing the game, however, it becomes very easy to slip into a worldly mentality that tells us we should strive to obtain all we can and make the most of our earthly lives while we are here. We have to endure this horrible world, so why not make the most of it?

This is precisely the mentality of people like Joel Osteen who focus all their attention on the things of this world rather than on the blessed hope of Christ. On page 33 of his book Osteen writes, "God wants you to live an overcoming life of victory. He doesn't want you to barely get by. He's called *El Shaddai*, 'the God of more than enough.' He's not 'El Cheapo,' the God of barely enough!"

The message here, like the rest in Osteen's book, is that God wants every believer to lead a rich, abundant life of luxury and prosperity. Like many people, Osteen misinterprets Jesus' promise in Matthew 6:33 that "all these things will be given to you" if you seek first God's kingdom and his righteousness. "All these things" is not referring to wealth, fame, or a reserved parking place at Walmart; it is referring to the necessities of life that Jesus mentions in the previous few verses. The reality is if God wanted every believer to possess material wealth, the Bible would not explicitly state that some believers are poor.

Proverbs 22:2 reads, "Rich and poor have this in common: The LORD is the Maker of them all." Likewise, James 2:5 says, "Listen, my dear brothers: Has not God chosen those who are poor in the eyes of the world to be rich in faith and to inherit the kingdom he promised those who love him?"

Often times, followers of Christ are regarded as poor by the world. In their meekness, charity, and humility, believers do not generally possess material wealth. Instead, they possess spiritual wealth as they are "rich in faith." Because of their allegiance to God and not the world, they are persecuted by the world but rejoice in the treasures they store up for themselves in heaven (Matthew 5:10-11, 6:19-20, 2 Timothy 3:12). The real inheritors of worldly wealth (the type Osteen and others seek and promote) are the wicked.

In Psalm 73:2-12, David laments the worldly riches of the wicked:

> But as for me, my feet had almost slipped; I had nearly lost my foothold. For I envied the arrogant when I saw the prosperity of the wicked. They have no struggles; their bodies are healthy and strong. They are free from the burdens common to man; they are not plagued by human ills. Therefore pride is their necklace; they clothe themselves with violence. From their callous hearts comes iniquity; the evil conceits of their minds know no limits. They scoff, and speak with malice; in their arrogance they threaten oppression. Their mouths lay claim to heaven, and their tongues take possession of the earth. Therefore their people turn to them and drink up waters in abundance. They say, "How can God know? Does the Most High have knowledge?" This is what the wicked are like—always carefree, they increase in wealth. (Psalm 73:2-12)

David uses words like "prosperity," "healthy," "strong," "carefree," and "wealth" to describe the earthly lives of wicked people. It's shocking how the lifestyle David attributes to sinners here is the exact type of lifestyle Joel Osteen and his cohorts promote for the body of Christ. The nice house, the fancy car, and the country club membership are all things David sees wicked men obtaining, not righteous men.

The riches of righteousness are very opposite those of this world. Wealth for a believer is not a million dollar home or a Rolls Royce—it is the reward reserved for him in heaven. His security is not financial, it is spiritual. His investments are in God's kingdom, not this temporal world.

Pastors like Joel Osteen are most likely aware of these truths but teach them anyway in an attempt to deceitfully flatter naïve masses. Osteen even admitted during a 60 Minutes television interview on October 14, 2007 that he is not gifted in understanding the Bible or teaching its meaning to his congregation! These are the types of people Paul warns against in Romans 16:17-18, where he writes, "I urge you, brothers, to watch out for those who cause divisions and put obstacles in your way that are contrary to the teaching you have learned. Keep away from them. For such people are not serving our Lord Christ, but their own appetites. By smooth talk and flattery they deceive the minds of naive people." In the same way, pastors like Osteen violate James 4:16 by boasting and bragging of their worldly accomplishments.

The tactics of such people are no different from those of Hitler when he brainwashed an entire nation or the Antichrist who will ultimately unite the world in deceitful flattery. While the message of *Your Best Life Now* may be appealing and motivating, it is ultimately dangerous. The idea that God's plan for our earthly lives is to bless us with material wealth and things of the world could not be further from the truth as we examine Scripture. Such heresy comes from the mouths of false teachers, wolves in sheep's clothing, or "blind guides" as Jesus calls them.

Be careful not to be fooled into believing such deception. According to God's Word, the harder your life is as a Christian, the more you know you are living a life for God and storing up treasures for yourself in heaven. Scripture makes it clear that hardship is inevitable for every believer and that our lives on earth will be riddled with trials. Take heart, though, for your best life is not "now," but is yet to come—and it's a whole lot better than the "best" this world has to offer!

Questions for Reflection

1. Are you one of the many Joel Osteen fans in America? If so, ask yourself why you are so drawn to his message.

2. When does the Bible say our "best life" is as Christians?

3. What are "all these things" Jesus refers to in Matthew 6:33? Does He mean worldly luxuries or the necessities of life?

4. What types of riches should we seek? Spiritual riches or riches of the world? Where should we invest and store our treasures?

15 | *Conclusion: "Semper Reformata!"*

Here we are at the end of the book, and I have no doubt that you have experienced moments of confusion, frustration, and even anger at many points throughout your reading. Perhaps your arsenal of Christian slogans includes all of the ones I mentioned in this book. Maybe it includes a few or possibly even none. Either way, your assumptions about the Bible were probably challenged in one way or another as you confronted the many deceptions addressed in this book, and I hope God revealed a great deal to you in your reading.

In the first chapter I extended a challenge to you. Like my friend, Tom, I offered to recant of the things I said in this book if you are able to provide me with solid Scriptural evidence to support the validity of what I have deemed fourteen heretical misconceptions. If you accepted my challenge, I ask now how successful you were in finding evidence to disprove my claims. Would you feel comfortable in a debate over any of the myths I raised in the book's fourteen chapters of deceptions?

My guess is that you did not find much evidence to refute my claims because such evidence does not exist (at least not in the

Bible.) Many of the fallacies I address do possess a certain degree of truth, but none of them are entirely true in a biblical context.

You may be wondering why I have gone to such lengths to expose simple misconceptions. Do these misunderstandings really affect our understanding of God or our relationship with Him? Are they really so significant that they warrant your time in reading this book?

The answer to those questions is yes, they affect those things a great deal and *are* worthy of your time. Proverbs 9:10 declares, "The fear of the LORD is the beginning of wisdom, and knowledge of the Holy One is understanding." The more we increase in our knowledge of God, the more we understand Him. The more we fear the Lord, the wiser we become.

The common denominator among all the misconceptions in this book is their attempt to put man in a position above God. They paint an inappropriate image of the Sovereign Master of the universe as a lenient, gentle, and completely tolerant deity who exists for man's pleasure. They focus on things of this world, rather than the blessings of Christ's kingdom.

The modern church is concerned above all else with growth in numbers before growth in righteousness. A pastor friend of mine once told me that he often dreamt of the chance to someday interview with a church board and reply to their inevitable question of whether or not he could grow their church with the antithetical promise, "I could grow your church from five hundred to fifty." You see, true growth lies in spiritual maturity, not mere numbers. Indeed, the more souls won for Christ the better, but it is just as important for us to ensure that those who already profess to be Christians are grounded firmly in their faith and their understanding of the Lord.

Throughout the book, you may have noticed that I often refer to potentially lost Christians as "professing Christians." I do this intentionally, not to make a mockery of them, but to suggest that such people may not truly be saved. Their understanding of God is so far removed from the truth that their salvation begs questioning. They may profess to be saved, but that is not concrete proof that they are. Pronouncing judgment on them is not our place, but ensuring that our brethren walk in the Spirit is our duty. The unfortunate reality is that questioning others, just like rebuking them, almost always leads to resentment and anger. The Bible tells us that truth will always see much more controversy in the world than falsity will. It has been said, "Error never wants to be challenged; truth will always desire examination." Someone else once quoted, "Truth can always stand the test of scrutiny. Error…always breeds tolerance."

This has been my theme while writing this book. The truths I expound here will no doubt attract a great deal of scrutiny, but that scrutiny is only further confirmation of their validity. If this work were erroneous, it would be fully accepted and never questioned.

You may be like I was—stubborn in my lack of understanding and unwilling to accept the truth. When my friend shared the truths of God's Word with me, I was offended, confused, and ready to give up on my faith altogether. Many Calvinists testify that their conversion was anything but pretty. A deacon I know always tells me that he came into Reformed Theology "kicking and screaming over a three year period."

God's ways are foolishness to us and it is not in our power to understand, let alone accept them without the divine inspiration of our merciful Father (1 Corinthians 1:18). All we can do is rely entirely on God and allow the Holy Spirit to continually sanctify us as we become increasingly holy.

The phrase *semper reformata* means "always reforming." The early Reformers like Martin Luther and John Calvin recognized the importance of continually reforming in our faith. The word *reform* means to alter, correct, or change for the better. So, by "always reforming" we are ensuring that we are keeping in step with the Spirit and staying on the straight and narrow path.

Often times this means tackling subjects that are a bit uncomfortable to some. Change is rarely ever easy, and it is no different when it comes to our faith. In fact, change in a spiritual sense is much more difficult than worldly change, and this is a reality that is stressed countless times in the Word of God.

The goal of this book is to spark a reformation. Like the Roman Catholic Church in Luther's time, the church today needs a dose of biblical truth injected into it. It needs an occasional reminder nailed to its door, and a few more Martin Luthers, John Calvins, and Jonathan Edwards's preaching from its pulpits. If the modern church understood the common fallacies of Christendom and committed itself to forsaking them, the body of Christ would be unified in a way like never before.

No doubt, many will not take kindly to biblical truth as the Bible itself predicts, but for those who accept the Word of God, there will be a spiritual conversion beyond anything they ever thought possible.

My sincere hope is that in reading this book you have grown closer to our Lord. Through a deeper understanding of your relationship with Christ and what it truly means to be a Christian, I am confident you will experience joy beyond measure and an awakening similar to mine that morning in Ohio. My hope is that all who read these words will heed them not with itching ears, but with open hearts and minds, eager to grow closer to Christ Jesus. For those who refute the truth of God's Word, I echo the words of Martin Luther: "Here I stand; I can do no other."

   Soli Deo Gloria.

Printed in the United States
96711LV00002B/93/A

9 781604 415544